WHEN *the* SKY FELL

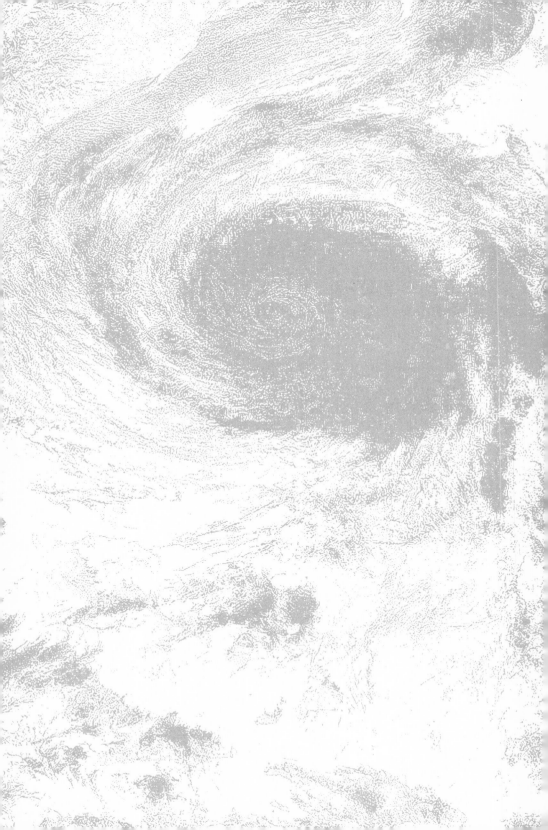

WHEN

the

SKY FELL

*Hurricane Maria and the
United States in Puerto Rico*

MICHAEL DEIBERT

APOLLO
PUBLISHERS

This book is dedicated to the memories of those who lost their lives during Hurricane Maria and its aftermath, and those who fought to save them. And to the memory of my grandfather James Breon.

CONTENTS

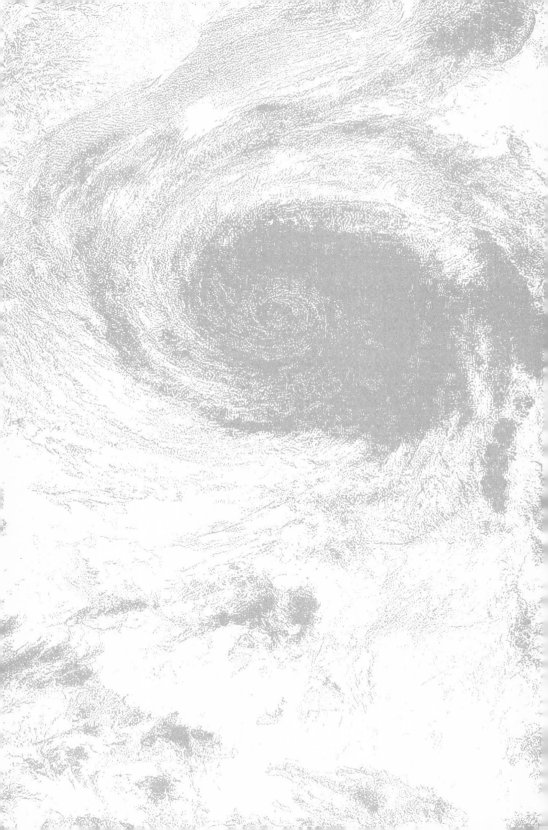

Be not afeard; the isle is full of noises,

Sounds and sweet airs, that give delight and hurt not.

Sometimes a thousand twangling instruments

Will hum about mine ears, and sometime voices

That, if I then had waked after long sleep,

Will make me sleep again: and then, in dreaming,

The clouds methought would open and show riches

Ready to drop upon me that, when I waked,

I cried to dream again.

—William Shakespeare, *The Tempest*

BARRANQUITAS

THE MAN TRUDGED UP THE ROAD, BEHIND HIM A VISTA OF UNDU-
lating mountains sloping green away in the distance. Between him and the
cordillera, the town's winding streets were studded with fallen utility poles
and power lines strewn along the road like confetti.

As he got closer I could see his weathered face, freed from a band of
shadow as the sun burned down through a cerulean sky. He held a walkie-
talkie in his hand that periodically erupted to life with messages delivered
in an urgent staccato crackle.

"What you are looking at is the work of five decades destroyed," the
man told me. His name was Francisco López, and for nearly twenty-one
years he had been the mayor of the town of Barranquitas, where we now
stood in the central mountains of Puerto Rico. "All the roads have been
damaged, six bridges have collapsed, around twelve hundred homes were
destroyed. Communication has basically been cut off. This is a critical
situation. We are working day and night to get back on our feet."

Three weeks earlier, Hurricane Maria, a Category 5 storm with winds of 160 miles per hour, had roared out of the Atlantic like a banshee chasing down its prey and had rent devastation on the island that few could have conceived of only days before. Under its wind and lashing rains, entire neighborhoods were destroyed, whole towns were cut off, and the young, sick, and otherwise vulnerable were left to largely fend for themselves in the midst of a pervasive absence of any help coming from the federal government on the mainland of the United States. I had arrived on the island a few days earlier, and a local photographer, Nydia Meléndez Rivas, and I had been driving around, taking stock and trying to document the destruction. On a meandering path along the coast from the capital, San Juan, we had passed through scenes of biblical devastation. Driving around Barranquitas, one saw the remnants of bridges resting in heaps at the bottom of ravines amid a backdrop of the fevered attempts by local officials to bring aid to those who needed it.

"Barranquitas was very affected and without water because the roads were very impacted, but little by little things are getting better," barrel-chested, mustachioed Sgt. José Oliveras of Puerto Rico's National Guard told me as private vehicles from the municipality came to a converted sports complex to deliver food and other necessities to those in need.

A little further down the road, a makeshift medical clinic had been set up by a Methodist church, and volunteers and doctors saw waves of people seeking medical attention. We wandered through the assemblage until we came upon Eileen Rivera Diaz, the wife of the pastor of the church where the clinic was being held.

"The services for people with medical complications, with cancer, diabetes, hypertension, lupus were very affected by the storm," she told us as we spoke on a back balcony that overlooked a lush valley, with dark clouds rolling menacingly on the horizon. "There is not a strong presence of the federal government here."

"There are a lot of neighborhoods here without access to medical care, to lights, to water, to medicines," Oscar Ruiz of the Sociedad Puertorriqueña de Endocrinología y Diabetología, whose group was traveling around the island conducting health clinics, told me. "We are trying to help, but there is a great need."

Though only dimly understood on the mainland, Puerto Rico's relationship with the United States had been the defining factor of its political life for more than a century. After four hundred years of Spanish rule, the United States seized the island from Spain in 1898 during the Spanish-American War. For the last 121 years, Puerto Rico has been an overseas territory of the United States, which some have seen as a boon of good fortune and others as relegating it to the status of a second-class colonial outpost. Its native-born residents are American citizens, but do not have a vote in the US Congress and cannot vote in general presidential elections. (This means that there is effectively no representation for Puerto Rico's population of nearly 3.2 million people. Wyoming, by contrast, has two US senators and a member of the House of Representatives while boasting a population of only around 580,000.)

I had something of a family history with Puerto Rico myself. Between 1971 and 1974, en route to Sunset Park, Brooklyn, from Argentina, my grandmother and my grandfather, a Lutheran minister, lived in the western city of Mayagüez, which my grandfather wrote about rhapsodically in his memoirs. In a two-bedroom apartment a block from the stadium where the Indios de Mayagüez baseball team played, and across the street from a sprawling *caserio* (as public housing projects are known on the island), my grandparents lived under the shade of a coconut palm and lime trees and gazed out on the spectacular sunsets above the Bahía de Mayagüez, just to the west, every night. My grandfather opened an after-school tutoring program for the children of the caserio in their apartment and walked through it nearly every day, learning a bit about people's lives. Even among the caserio's roughest delinquents, he said he never felt threatened, and spoke frequently about the intense natural beauty of the island.

In many ways, Barranquitas was a unique town. It had been the birthplace of Luis Muñoz Rivera, a journalist, poet, and politician who had been one of the towering figures in the island's political life of the late nineteenth and early twentieth centuries, and who had served as Puerto Rico's resident commissioner—as the elected but nonvoting member of the United States House of Representatives is called—from 1911 to 1916. The Jones–Shafroth Act, which was crafted with significant input from Don Luis, as Muñoz Rivera was known, and which granted US citizenship to most Puerto Ricans, would come into effect only months after his sudden death in November 1916. Decades later, his son, Luis Muñoz Marín, would pick up the family's political mantle, serving as governor from 1949 to 1965 and ushering the island into its Estado Asociado Libre (Free Associated State) hybrid status vis-à-vis the United States. Commonly referred to as a commonwealth, this status deepened what many saw as the island's quasi-colonial relationship with the giant nation to its north, and continues to this day. Puerto Ricans became US citizens who could travel back and forth to the mainland at will. They could vote in party primaries during US presidential elections but not in the general election itself. They could—and did—fight in comparatively large numbers in the armed forces during US conflicts abroad, but a swath of islanders viewed the US presence itself as little more than a military occupation with social-democratic window dressing.

And where was that great power now? Around Barranquitas, I looked in vain for some sign of a US government presence, finally finding one at a Federal Emergency Management Agency (FEMA) disaster recovery center—one of only five extant on this island the size of Connecticut—where around one hundred people from the region waited to be seen. FEMA would see residents "on an individual case-by-case basis," the center manager told me.

"Not everyone has the same problems, the same damages, or the same income." he explained, during a cigarette break behind the recreation center in which he and a single other employee were working. When I asked him about the difficulty of residents applying for aid, given the fact that virtually all phone communication and electricity on the island had collapsed, he told me, "We're doing what we always do, we're urging people, if they can't get to us, to apply online or over the phone."

Beyond Barranquitas, the road between the towns of Comerío and Naranjito, in the direction toward the capital, from which aid would likely come, appeared on the verge of collapse in various places, with one lane of the two-lane pass having collapsed down the mountainside. Houses along the road were filled floor to ceiling with a thick red clay that had burst through their windows in an apparent landslide. As Nydia and I made our way gingerly along the mountainside, we saw a white-haired woman standing forlornly at her front gate.

"I'm eighty years old, I've lived in this house for fifty years, and I've never seen anything like this," Aida Jiménez told me as she stood in the shell of her home overlooking a green valley, a tiny kitten darting around her feet. "Look at my house, it's gone, many of the other houses, too. And most of the island, actually."

As she spoke, the wind from the dark clouds we had seen rolling in earlier began to pick up, causing the shell of her house to sigh mournfully in the breeze. In the valley below, one could see a tattered, faded piece of fabric above another damaged home. As the rain approached, it flapped defiantly in the breeze. It was the flag of Puerto Rico.

1

THE ENCHANTED ISLAND

HOW BEAUTIFUL IT MUST HAVE BEEN.

A little over one hundred miles from east to west at its widest point and forty miles from north to south, the island we now call Puerto Rico was splashed by the blue-green Caribbean and climbed from coastal lowlands to lush tropical mountain forests. The island was dotted with fauna and the waters around it brimmed with fish. The people who are now referred to as Tainos once referred to themselves based on the names of the locales where they lived, and those who lived on Puerto Rico referred to themselves as *Bonrinquen*, after their name for the island itself. They lived in large, settled villages governed by a cacique (chief), with extended families living in round dwellings with conical roofs arranged around a central plaza. Rule by district caciques existed under regional caciques, and the Taino class structure was more or less divided between nobility and commoners. The Tainos crafted delicate work out of gold that they mined, as well as out of wood, stone, and bone. The Taino approach to agriculture was fairly refined, with cassava and sweet potatoes representing their main root crops, grown in permanent fields along with fruits, cotton, and tobacco, and they maintained a variety of fishing methods that included nets, spears, and poison. They worshipped deities known as *zenmi,* the chief of which were Atabey, the goddess of fresh water and fertility, and her son, Yúcahu, the god of cassava and the sea.[1]

On November 19, 1493, on his second voyage to the Americas, the Italian explorer Christopher Columbus landed on Puerto Rico and christened the island San Juan Bautista in honor of St. John the Baptist. As his men roamed around neighboring Quisqueya (which he renamed La Isla Española, thereafter largely known as Hispaniola, and where present-day Haiti and the Dominican Republic reside), Columbus seems to have treated Puerto Rico as something of an afterthought. That changed when, fresh from participating in a massacre of indigenous Tainos in Higüey while under the command of Nicolás de Ovando y Cáceres in what is now the eastern Dominican Republic, Juan Ponce de León was sent across the Mona Channel to exploit the goldfields that had been discovered there. Ponce de León helped to found two settlements: Caparra, the first European settlement on the territory, was built within the limits of what is present-day Guaynabo in 1508, followed by San Germán in the western mountains. (By 1521, the village of Caparra had moved to the site of present-day Old San Juan.)[2] Eventually, the phrase applied to the northern bay, *puerto rico* (rich port), was extended to the entire island. The most powerful cacique initially encountered by the Spanish was Agüeybaná, whose relations with the Spaniards were initially cordial, if guarded.

But the Spaniards certainly did not view the Taino as anything remotely approaching their equals. As the historian Carrie Gibson has noted, from the Spanish perspective, "here were slaves to capture and people to convert."[3] What followed was a holocaust. The number of indigenous people slaughtered during the Spanish conquest of the Caribbean was estimated by Bartolomé de las Casas to be more than twelve million.[4] As elsewhere, the *encomienda* system of communal slavery of the indigenous inhabitants was practiced in Puerto Rico.[5] Following Agüeybaná's death, his brother, Agüeybaná II, staged an uprising in 1511—the same year the Spanish friar Antonio de Montesinos denounced the *encomienda* system during an impassioned sermon in Santo Domingo[6]—which saw the killing of several hundred Spaniards. Ponce de León responded to the revolt with what amounted to ethnic cleansing, with smallpox largely finishing off the job the Spaniards had started.[7] By the 1530s, the goldfields in Puerto Rico were exhausted.[8] The Spaniards then turned their attention to an equally terrible system.

In 1510, around 250 Africans would be shipped to the Caribbean under the authorization of King Ferdinand.[9] Tens of thousands would rapidly follow. Between 1766 and 1770, a single company—the Compañía Aguirre-Aróstegui—imported at least ten thousand slaves. Between 1780 and 1795, the slave population in Puerto Rico increased from 11,250 to 18,053.[10] The slaves brought with them aspects of their culture that were not so easily erased, however; for example, the *baile de bomba*, as it became known, featured singing and dancing and a mélange of African, Spanish, and non-Spanish Caribbean influences and was often suspected of having potentially subversive or revolutionary components by the island's planter class. Even after the end of slavery some municipalities attempted (without much success) to legislate against it.[11]

The island proved a tempting target for the privateers traversing Caribbean waters. In August 1595, the English pirate Francis Drake and a force of about twenty-five hundred men departed Plymouth aboard twenty-seven ships bound for the Spanish Caribbean. Drake was around fifty-five years old, an old age for the era, "though still alert and capable of physical vigor,"[12] and was returning to the scene of some of his greatest glories. After a disastrous attempt to resupply his fleet at Grand Canary, the fleet proceeded at a glacial pace, dallying for days in Guadeloupe before proceeding. This greatest of pirates was slower and less impetuous than in his younger days, and the Spanish had seen them coming. By the time Drake and his men finally made their assault on San Juan in mid-November, the Spanish flooded the city with men and artillery that rained down on the British, killing about forty of Drake's men before sending him packing to Panama, where he died from ignoble dysentery only weeks later.[13] Between Drake's final assault and 1703, the island would be attacked eight more times by English, French, and Dutch forces.[14]

For much of the first two centuries after its initial conquest by the Spanish, Puerto Rico remained little more than a glorified military outpost, with only two population centers of any notable size—present-day San Juan, and San Germán in the western mountains. Eventually large cattle-raising estates, known as *hatos*, enclosed smaller plots of land and existed in conditions of perfect feudalism, rights to their exploitation handed down by colonial municipal councils in San Juan and San Germán.[15] The Puerto Rican writer Tomás Blanco described the beginning of the island as "this small number of neighbors, grouped in the shadow of an imperial fortress [and] a military prison," while adding "notwithstanding the chronic poverty of the island, its inhabitants managed to satisfy their needs and desires quite well, without great effort, adapting to the climate and all the products of heaven."[16]

By the mid-1700s, however, things began to change dramatically. In less than four decades between 1765 and 1802, the island's population grew by 264 percent.[17] In the decade between 1817 and 1827, the island's exportation of sugar increased 680 percent.[18] The rapid growth of sugar plantations, particularly on the coastal plains, forced thousands of subsistence farmers from their homes and into the heretofore sparsely populated interior.[19] In the early part of the nineteenth century, Ponce, Mayagüez, and Guayama had formed a triumvirate of centers for sugar-based agriculture performed by slaves.[20] Decades later, in a letter to Spanish authorities, Governor Segundo de la Portilla Gutiérrez would confess that slavery had been "the medullary nerve of production" on the sugar plantations.[21]

One of the key architects of this policy was the Spanish colonial governor Miguel de la Torre, who served in that role from 1822 until 1837. Arriving on the island to assume his post with his defeat at the hands of Venezuela's Simón Bolívar at the Battle of Carabobo behind him, he was wary of the possibility of rebellion. In addition to his rapid expansion of the sugar industry, he adopted a police he referred to as *baile, botella, y baraja* (drinking, dancing, and cards), and supported some cultural initiatives (such as the building of the Teatro Municipal), while ruling with a brutal hand in the political sphere. By the early 1800s, free blacks outnumbered slaves in Puerto Rico by almost half the total population.[22] Towns such as Loíza would become important centers of Afro-Puerto Rican culture. With Haiti's January 1804 declaration of victory over the French, slavery as it had been known ceased to exist on the western third of Hispaniola. In the present-day Dominican Republic, slavery was temporarily abolished during the Haitian uprising, only to be reinstated in 1809 by Spain, and then finally abolished again during Haiti's twenty-year occupation of the area by Haitian president Jean-Pierre Boyer. In August 1834, slavery was abolished throughout the British Empire. In Cuba and Puerto Rico, however, the struggle to finally end the system would continue for decades more.

The contemporaneous writing of firsthand observers such as the Spanish Benedictine monk Fray Íñigo Abbad y Lasierra, who arrived on the island in 1771, seemed to depict a vaguely louche life of abundance and tropical torpor for those who lorded over the island's slave economy. In San Juan, he found a city "embellished with trees and plants, which grow between the houses, forming a forest. . . . For the most part, the people are fed with the fruits of their crops, but they do not stop spending a lot on flour, wine, oil, brandy, olives, cheeses, hams and other foreign foods."[23] In 1812, the Constitution of Cádiz made Puerto Rico a province of Spain, with all the attendant rights associated with that status, before it was quickly reversed, reinstated, and reversed again in a whiplash swing of the political compass that, by 1824, saw the island again under direct Spanish rule.[24]

Events beyond Puerto Rico's shores, however, were profoundly reorienting the balance of global power. In December 1823, in a message to the US Congress, US President James Monroe declared that

> The American continents, by the free and independent condition
> which they have assumed and maintain, are henceforth not to be
> considered as subjects for future colonization by any European powers.
> . . . With the Governments who have declared their independence
> and maintained it, and whose independence we have, on great
> consideration and on just principles, acknowledged, we could not view
> any interposition for the purpose of oppressing them, or controlling in
> any other manner their destiny, by any European power in any other
> light than as the manifestation of an unfriendly disposition toward the
> United States.[25]

The ascendant United States was telling Europe in no uncertain terms that its days of intervening in the western hemisphere at will were over. Less than two decades later, in 1854, the Franco-American politician and diplomat Pierre Soulé, formerly a senator from Louisiana and then serving as US envoy to Spain, served as the driving force behind what became known as the Ostend Manifesto (taking its name from the town in Belgium where Soulé met envoy to France John Y. Mason and envoy to Great Britain James Buchanan to discuss how to acquire the island of Cuba). The document argued that the United States should purchase Cuba from Spain—a move that would have greatly benefited slave-owning states in the US—and declare war on Spain if the latter refused the offer. When Soulé incautiously allowed word of the plot to leak out, the plan was roundly denounced by many European powers and by antislavery forces within the US.

In the interim, with Spain's empire increasingly enfeebled by political battles at home (between 1833 and 1892, Spain had seventy-five separate governments), the 1831 creation of the Real Audiencia de Puerto Rico granted the island its own judiciary within a system that had previously been administered first from Santo Domingo and then from Cuba. In the decade following the Ostend Manifesto, the Union Army's annihilation of the Confederacy during the US Civil War forced many to see the writing on the wall for the rest of the hemisphere, with the Spanish parliamentarian Antonio María Fabié observing that "the war in the United States is finished and, being finished, slavery on the whole American continent can be taken as finished."[26]

By the late 1860s, though, the Caribbean was again in tumult. The caudillo Pedro Santana had connived in the Dominican Republic to cede control of that portion of Hispaniola back to Spain as a means to preserve his own autocratic rule, which in turn led to the Guerra de la Restauración (Restoration War). The war raged in the country from 1863 to 1865, resulting in the expulsion of Spanish troops from a largely devastated nation full of prowling armed bands. Anxious to avoid a repeat of such a fiasco, following their defeat the Spanish rulers of Puerto Rico sought to liberalize its political system, a move that proved too little, too late for many.

As in Cuba, rebellion on the island had been brewing for some time and out of the firmament emerged the figure of Ramón Emeterio Betances, a French-educated doctor who, while a student in Paris, had witnessed the tumultuous Révolution de Février (February Revolution) uprising, which resulted in the creation of the French Second Republic. He returned to his native island full of vigor to dynamite it out of what he viewed as its medieval torpor. The son of a mixed-race immigrant from Hispaniola who eventually succeeded in *limpieza de sangre* (literally "cleaning the blood") on the national registry to thereafter be considered white,[27] Betances was an abolitionist and Pan-Caribbeanist who translated a biography of the Haitian revolutionary leader Toussaint Louverture into Spanish.[28]

By the middle of the 1860s, many of Puerto Rico's independence leaders were in exile, most in the United States but some in the Dominican Republic. In January 1867, the exiled patriots formed the Comité

Revolucionario de Puerto Rico (Revolutionary Committee of Puerto Rico) to push for the independence of both Puerto Rico and Cuba from Spain. The committee included Betances, the abolitionist Segundo Ruiz Belvis, Juan Ríus Rivera, and José Francisco Basora (like Betances, a physician). Knowing the power of the pen, Betances authored pro-independence tracts such as the *Diez Mandamientos de los Hombres Libres* (Ten Commandments of Free Men), which circulated around the island and advocated such steps as "abolition of slavery," "freedom of speech," and "the right to own weapons."[29] Similarly, the poet Lola Rodríguez de Tió—who would write that Cuba and Puerto Rico were so close in struggle that they were like *de un pájaro las dos alas*[30] (two wings of the same bird)—added patriotic lyrics to the already-popular tune of *La Borinqueña*. A revolutionary flag was created by the *independentista* Mariana Bracetti, and armed cells led by figures such as New Orleans-born Mathias Brugman and Venezuelan-born Manuel Rojas—both of whom considered the island their home and had become strong patriots—began to form clandestinely. On September 23, 1868, hundreds of rebels gathered at Rojas's hacienda near Lares in the central-west mountains before entering the town in a shambolic fashion after nightfall and declaring a republic.

The rebellion—which became known as *el Grito de Lares* (the Cry of Lares)—quickly fizzled, however, and many of the rebel leaders and supporters were rounded up by Spanish authorities. All those arrested were sentenced to death, but the following year, a new governor, José Laureano Sanz y Posse, declared a general amnesty leading to the release of all the prisoners. Betances, who was not in Puerto Rico at the time of the revolt, spent many subsequent years still organizing, but in largely disappointed exile in New York and the Dominican Republic, for whom he eventually became a diplomat. Subsequent years in France saw him awarded the *Légion d'honneur*, and he died in Neuilly-sur-Seine in September 1898.

Though in many ways Puerto Rico served as a mere sideshow to the final Cuban wars of independence, the behavior of the colonialist forces on the larger island gave a flavor for the kind of savagery the Spanish were capable of against their citizens, in some ways presaging the slaughter of Spain's own 1936 to 1939 civil war. Sent to Cuba at the beginning of the Guerra de los Diez Años (Ten Years' War), which erupted in 1868 only a month after the Lares uprising, General Valeriano Weyler organized a group of fanatical pro-Spanish volunteers to fight rebels such as those loyal to Antonio Maceo and Máximo Gómez. These troops made little distinction between rebels and Cuban civilians and became notorious for returning from battle carrying the heads of their opponents by the hair. After being appointed governor general in January 1896, Weyler conducted a campaign utterly unmoored to the rules of war, slaughtering rebels and civilians alike and herding Cubans into compounds under armed guard to starve and die of disease in what many have described as a genocide against the local population, as over one hundred thousand people perished in the camps.[31]

In Puerto Rico, meanwhile, following el Grito de Lares, as the result of fierce lobbying by Madrid-educated botanist Román Baldorioty de Castro, veteran military man Luis Padial, and author Julio Vizcarrondo, among others, the Moret Law, named after the Spanish politician Segismundo Moret, was adopted on July 4, 1870. It granted partial abolition for slaves in Puerto Rico and Cuba, granting freedom to slaves born after September 17, 1868, as well as those who were over sixty years old, had served in the Spanish army, or were property of the Spanish government. Full abolition would arrive in Puerto Rico three years later.[32]

With the existence of political parties on the island legalized,[33] the political debate coalesced around two main currents of thought, one of which advocated a further assimilation within the Spanish system, and the other of which pushed for increasing self-determination for the island's citizens. The arrival of the liberal Gabriel Baldrich y Palau as governor gave further oxygen to this opening of political space. Baldorioty de Castro would help found the Partido Liberal Reformista—the first political party on the island—in 1870 to advocate for the decentralized approach that encompassed both those who wanted to create their own autonomous government on the island and those who defended reforms within the Spanish system, while the awkwardly named Partido Liberal Conservador pushed for continued ties with Spain (it would eventually rename itself the Partido Incondicional Español).[34] The situation in Spain itself continued to be one of great tumult, with the brief, progressive First Spanish Republic (February 1873 to December 1874) ending with the restoration of the monarchy and a corrupt political duopoly between conservative and liberal factions there.

In late 1886, Baldorioty de Castro held a mass meeting at the Teatro La Perla in Ponce where more than seven hundred attendees debated what would become the Plan de Ponce, a political program that pushed for a range of reforms, including universal suffrage, individual rights, the rights to freedom of worship and freedom of expression, and a republican form of government. On the foundation of the Partido Liberal Reformista, the aging Baldorioty de Castro would form the Partido Autonomista Puertorriqueño with a group of younger, dynamic political actors. These included Dr. José Celso Barbosa Alcala, a University of Michigan-educated Afro-Puerto Rican physician and sociologist from Bayamón, and a pair of journalist-poets: José de Diego, the son of a Spanish army officer, and Barranquitas native Luis Muñoz Rivera, a son of the island's middle class whose paternal grandfather had been a career military man and fought in the *Campaña Admirable* against Simón Bolívar before arriving in Puerto Rico with his commanding officer (and later the island's Spanish governor) Miguel de la Torre.

As the autonomist movement began to garner more support, Spain's military governor, Romualdo Palacios González, responded by launching a series of raids against *autonomista* leaders in August 1887, leading to the jailing of dozens, including Baldorioty de Castro (he would die only two years later). Some of those arrested were subjected to torture.[35] Once Palacios González was removed, the Partido Autonomista continued to advocate for greater autonomy through peaceful means.

The old rebel spirit had not been entirely extinguished, however. In March 1897, nearly thirty years after el Grito de Lares, another revolt against Spanish rule erupted, this one centered on the southwestern town of Yauco. Led by local coffee baron Antonio Mattei Lluberas, who visited New York to plot with the exiled Ramón Emeterio Betances, this uprising lasted for only a few days in late March, and became known rather dispiritingly as the *Intentona de Yauco* (Attempted Coup of Yauco); those arrested were granted amnesty and released at the end of the year. On the economic front, the rise of coffee in the late 1890s led to Ponce entering a golden era during which it nearly rivaled San Juan.[36]

The amnesty given to the putschists was a sign of changing political winds in Spain itself. In November 1897, the Carta Autonómica de Puerto Rico, together with a similar measure for Cuba, was proposed by Spain's liberal prime minister Práxedes Mateo Sagasta, and signed into law by Queen María Cristina. It granted Puerto Rico significant autonomy in terms of legislation (establishing an elected thirty-two member Chamber of Representatives), the judiciary, and a large amount of economic control.[37] Elections for the Chamber of Representatives would be held in March 1898 amid an atmosphere of tenuous hope.[38] Tomás Blanco would later call the Carta Autonómica "the crystallization, long claimed and debated, of a state of law that opened a wide channel to the hope of resolving regional problems from a local point of view."[39] The new century seemed to beckon, so close and so full of promise after so many years of hard struggle.

2

IN THE SHADOW OF EMPIRE

In November 1897, Theodore Roosevelt, then assistant secretary of the Navy in the administration of President William McKinley, sat down at his desk in Washington, DC, and penned a letter to the Navy officer William Kimball, one of the strongest proponents of modernizing the nation's capacity for naval warfare.

> I would regard a war with Spain from two standpoints. First, the advisability on the grounds both of humanity and self-interest of interfering on behalf of the Cubans, and of taking one more step toward the complete freeing of America from European dominion; second, the benefit done our people by giving them something to think of which is not material gain, and especially the benefit done our military forces by trying both the Navy and Army in actual practice.[40]

Roosevelt had only been at his post for seven months, but he had already emerged as one of the driving forces for war within the McKinley government. Holding a strange, almost mystical vision of combat, Roosevelt had long been haunted by his own father's failure to fight during the American Civil War, and had longed to prove his mettle during a similar conflict. He would soon get his chance.

Just before 10:00 p.m. on the evening of February 15, 1898, an explosion tore through the battleship USS Maine as it sat in the harbor in Havana, where it had been sent to safeguard US economic interests as the war between Cuban rebels and the government of Spain continued to rage. Some 266 sailors perished as a result of the disaster, which a Navy inquiry concluded was caused by a mine (two subsequent inquiries would conclude the cause was an explosion of ammunition within the ship itself). A number of prominent newspapers in the United States, including those owned by William Randolph Hearst and Joseph Pulitzer, affixed blame to Spain, albeit with scant evidence to back their claims up. The battle cry "Remember the Maine!" became an immutable detail of the steady march to war.[41]

On April 11, McKinley delivered what became known as his "War Message" to Congress, in which he mentioned the Maine and called Spain's war in Cuba one of "subjugation or extermination." Going on to list a variety of economic and humanitarian justifications for war with Spain, he said he had determined that

> The forcible intervention of the United States as a neutral to stop the war, according to the large dictates of humanity and following many historical precedents where neighboring states have interfered to check the hopeless sacrifices of life by internecine conflicts beyond their borders, is justifiable on rational grounds.[42]

An amendment by Colorado Republican Senator Henry M. Teller to the joint resolution by Congress in response to McKinley's statement mandated that, following the cessation of hostilities with Spain, the United

States "leave the government and control of the island to its people."[43]

Puerto Rico often seemed to be treated as something of a mere detail to the larger war the United States would fight. Teller himself believed that Puerto Ricans were "not fighters like the Cubans. They were under Spanish tyranny for centuries without showing enough manhood to oppose it. Such a race does not deserve citizenship."[44] Alabama senator John Tyler Morgan, a former slave owner and staunch segregationist who was a major force on the Senate Foreign Relations Committee at the time, set forth the view that while the island was "too small" to be independent, it was nevertheless too strategically important to be left for others to rule.[45] The *New York Times* opined that

> There is no reason why it should not become a veritable garden of the tropics and an especially charming Winter resort for denizens of the North. Apart from the attractions of climate and scenery, there is a quaint picturesqueness in the old Spanish towns, and many interesting associations with the infancy of America.... There are neglected opportunities for the study of American ethnology in the island, as well as political, naval, and commercial advantages to be gained, and infinite attractions of tropic scenery and climate to be visited.[46]

The liberal reforms for Puerto Rico contained in the Carta Autonómica and the elections that had just been held for the island's Chamber of Representatives were thrown into chaos when, on May 12, 1898, a US fleet under the command of Rear Admiral William T. Sampson began bombarding San Juan in the first salvo of its impending invasion of the island. After firing 1,362 shells, killing two Spanish soldiers, injuring more than thirty, and losing one of its own number, the US fleet returned to Cuba.[47] They would not be away for long.

To lead the invasion of Puerto Rico, McKinley chose General Nelson A. Miles, a former Union Army officer who had fought at Antietam,

Chancellorsville (where he was shot twice), and Spotsylvania before leading a scorched-earth campaign against Native Americans on the Great Plains. Miles and his forces landed at Guánica, in the southwest of the island, on July 25, 1898. Miles became the first in a series of US military governors who would rule the island for the next two years. Three days after landing, Miles issued a proclamation to the island's residents which read, in part,

> In the prosecution of the war against the kingdom of Spain by the people of the United States, in the cause of liberty, justice, and humanity, its military forces have come to occupy the island of Puerto Rico. They come bearing the banner of freedom, inspired by a noble purpose to seek the enemies of our country and yours, and to destroy or capture all who are in armed resistance. They bring you the fostering arm of a free people, whose greatest power is in its justice and humanity to all those living within its fold. . . . We have not come to make war upon the people of a country that for centuries has been oppressed, but, on the contrary, to bring you protection, not only to yourselves, but to your property; to promote your prosperity, and bestow upon you the immunities and blessings of the liberal institutions of our government. . . . This is not a war of devastation, but one to give all within the control of its military and naval forces the advantages and blessings of enlightened civilization.[48]

In many ways, the United States' invasions of Cuba and Puerto Rico marked the opening shot in the coming decades of American military adventurism in the hemisphere, and so pleased the powers-that-be in Washington that it prompted Secretary of State John Hay to write to Theodore Roosevelt (who had resigned as assistant secretary of the Navy to personally take part—at age thirty-nine—in the fighting in Cuba) congratulating him on his "splendid little war" in the Caribbean.[49]

In addition to Cuba and Puerto Rico, the United States would invade

Nicaragua in 1912 and occupy it with forces of varying size—setting its political course through force of arms—more or less continuously until 1933, at which point it left and bequeathed the country to the tender mercies of dictator Anastasio Somoza García, who had risen through the ranks of the Guardia Nacional the US had created. Somoza's family would rule the country until the overthrow of his son Anastasio Somoza Debayle in 1979. Following the overthrow and murder of President Vilbrun Guillaume Sam, the US occupied Haiti from 1915 to 1934, seizing government funds and putting them into an account under Navy control and spiriting the central bank's entire gold reserve away to the vaults of City Bank in New York. The US also established the Gendarmerie d'Haïti, which would eventually form the core of the reborn Haitian army.[50] From 1916 to 1924, the US would occupy the Dominican Republic, separated from Puerto Rico only by the Mona Channel, installing a series of American military governors until 1922 and, as in Nicaragua, creating a Guardia Nacional that would serve as a vehicle for a dictator, in this case Rafael Trujillo, to eventually take over the country (Trujillo ruled from 1930 until his assassination in 1961). And over the next two decades the US would occupy Cuba no less than three separate times, first as a direct military government from 1898 until 1902, then from 1906 to 1909, and again during what became known as the Sugar Intervention between 1917 and 1922.

Despite the promises of benevolence and munificence, many saw an ill omen for the occupation when the San Ciriaco hurricane devastated Puerto Rico on August 8, 1899, a little over a year after US troops had landed. Sixty miles wide, its eye took six hours to cross the island as it battered it with one-hundred-mile-per-hour winds, leveling homes in the cities, tearing crops and the humble *bohío* shacks the *jíbaros*—as the island's hardscrabble mountain peasants were known—lived in asunder in the rural areas, and sending walls of water crashing over islanders from churning rivers and the sea. In Ponce alone, five hundred died, most of them drowned. The mountain town of Utuado was particularly badly hit. In the mountains surrounding it, some starved as they sought out aid. Around the island, some two hundred people were rendered homeless. The *Boletín mercantil de Puerto Rico* bemoaned the fact that even as "all efforts to reconquer its previous normality" after the Spanish-American War and the rapid change of colonial masters on the island "were successively and fatally failing, an extremely violent hurricane . . . intensified the measure of its pains, immersing it in the most horrendous ruin and destroying the last hope for its salvation and welfare."

As the rain continued lightly once the hurricane had passed, Gervasio García Díaz, the interim mayor of Caguas, watched people emerge from their places of shelter, light candles by the roadside, and pray to be spared another storm, resembling, in his words, "skeletons leaving the grave."[51] Despite the fundamentally undemocratic nature of the US presence on the island, McKinley worked hard and quickly to stem the human suffering as a result of the storm, rapidly approving the distribution of food by US military personnel and appealing to mayors in major US cities to act with "the highest considerations of honor and good faith . . . [and give] a generous response to the demand of Puerto Rican distress." His efforts would stand in stark contrast to the example that would be set by another US leader years later.[52]

As one could imagine, the US invasion prompted a reordering of the local political scene. From the ashes of Román Baldorioty de Castro's Partido Autonomista, Dr. José Celso Barbosa Alcala formed the Partido Republicano de Puerto Rico on July 4, 1899. The Afro-Puerto Rican Barbosa Alcala considered the US Republican Party, as many did at the time, the party that ended slavery in the US, and thus saw it as a logical home for someone like himself, but his party adopted a curiously submissive position toward the rule of the island by a US Congress to which it had little recourse for appeal.[53] In October of the same year, Luis Muñoz Rivera founded the short-lived Partido Federal (PF) with other refugees from the

Partido Autonomista to urge for greater self-rule in reaction to the island's military regime.

Following the US invasion, labor moved into the political arena in a way it had not under the Spanish. The island's first union, the Federación Regional de Trabajadores (FRT), fell apart amid internal squabbling (a precursor of things to come) and would be eclipsed by a new entity, the Federación Libre de Trabajadores (FLT).[54] The labor organizer and feminist Luisa Capetillo played an important role in the FLT's early days and helped sensitize it to the cause of women's suffrage as a key component of its struggle. Around the same time, a Galician-born labor organizer resident in Puerto Rico, Santiago Iglesias Pantín, who had been active in the FLT, formed the Partido Socialista (PS), and seemed to see statehood as a possible balm to what he saw as the rapacious instincts of the island's propertied class. By 1901, under his leadership, the FLT voted to affiliate itself with the Federación Americana de los Trabajadores, the American Federation of Labor Unions (AFL), a move which, as César Ayala and Rafael Bernabe noted in their 2007 history of Puerto Rico, was "not conducive to a radical questioning of US political structures."[55] (The PS, however, would become a considerable political force, winning 14 percent of the vote in 1917 and 23.4 percent in 1920.[56])

The nuances of local Puerto Rican political competitions were, however, lost on many Americans, not least of all those who wielded the greatest power over the island's inhabitants. The prevailing view of many in the US concerning those they were to govern can be summed up in the following passage of a report military governor George Whitefield Davis sent in 1900:

> Many of the Southern States of the Union are proceeding
> to disenfranchise the illiterate colored population. . . . If the
> disenfranchisement of the negro illiterates of the Union can be
> justified, the same in Puerto Rico can be defended on equally good

grounds, for the educational, social and industrial status of a large portion of the native inhabitants of Puerto Rico is no higher than that of the colored people.

"There are, however," Davis conceded grudgingly, "a few well-educated Puerto Rican negroes, and some who own considerable property."[57]

The situation would scarcely improve with the advent of civilian rule. Former assistant secretary of the Navy and Massachusetts representative Charles Herbert Allen, the first civilian selected to rule the island as governor in May 1900, wrote in his first report home to McKinley that "the introduction of fresh blood is needed . . . the American capitalist . . . will come here not only with his capital but with the push and energy which always accompany his undertakings." Allen went on to assert that the island "will add to our national pride to see its riches developed and made of benefit to the world at large, by the indomitable thrift and industry which have always marked the pathway of the Anglo-Saxon."[58] Taking his own advice to heart, after serving a year as governor, Allen went on to create the American Sugar Refining Company, the largest sugar syndicate in the world, which would eventually become Domino Sugar, and which maintained extensive holdings throughout Puerto Rico.[59] As the coming years would prove, Puerto Rico had become fertile ground for the sons of gentlemen from the continental United States to come and seek their fortunes.

In April 1900, the US Congress enacted the Organic Act of 1900. Popularly known as the Foraker Act after its main sponsor, Ohio Republican Senator Joseph Foraker, the legislation is believed to have been largely crafted by William McKinley's secretary of war, Elihu Root, and enshrined a patently antidemocratic form of governance for the island. While granting some concessions to local voices, the new "system" differed little in substance from direct military rule. The island would heretofore be ruled by a governor and an eleven-member executive council, all appointed by the president of the United States. A thirty-five member House of Representatives would be elected, a court system—including a Supreme Court (also appointed) and United States District Court—would be designed, and a nonvoting resident commissioner (who was required to "read and write the English language") would be sent to the US Congress. All US federal laws would be enforceable on the island. The act stated that all legal proceedings in the judicial district of Puerto Rico (or "Porto Rico," as the US government insisted on continuing to spell it) "shall be conducted in the English language."[60]

While the Treaty of Paris would end the Spanish-American War on December 10, 1898, the United States would continue to occupy Cuba with a provisional military government until May 1902. Also significantly, the Platt Amendment, introduced by Connecticut Republican Senator Orville Platt and passed as part of the 1901 Army Appropriations Bill in March of that year, deepened, rather than alleviated, the dynamic of colonial domination between the United States and Spain's former colonies. It dictated that that the United States could intervene in Cuba militarily at any time "for the preservation of Cuban independence, the maintenance of a government adequate for the protection of life, property, and individual liberty, and for discharging the obligations with respect to Cuba imposed by the treaty of Paris on the United States." Additionally, Cuba ceded the Isla de Pinos "title thereto being left to future adjustment by treaty," and the government of Cuba was obligated to "sell or lease to the United States lands necessary for coaling or naval stations at certain specified points to be agreed upon with the President of the United States."[61] The 1903 Cuban–American Treaty of Relations would enshrine these conditions into law.

Needless to say, the citizens of Puerto Rico took note of these developments.

On September 6, 1901, William McKinley was shot by Leon Czolgosz, a Polish-American anarchist, while attending the Pan-American Exposition in Buffalo, New York. He died eight days later and was succeeded by

Theodore Roosevelt. Following the Spanish-American War, Washington had grown ever more assertive about what it viewed as its rightful dominance of the hemisphere. The previous year, a crisis in Venezuela saw the US Navy threaten war with Germany following a blockade that the latter, the United Kingdom, and Italy had imposed against the government of President Cipriano Castro. Hard as it may be to believe today, at the end of the nineteenth and outset of the twentieth centuries, Germany was looked upon as a serious hemispheric threat by the Americans, and with good reason. In 1897, Kaiser Wilhelm II had ordered his military advisers to draw up plans to invade the United States. They did.[62]

In Roosevelt's December 1904 State of the Union speech to Congress, he threw down a gauntlet that became known as the Roosevelt Corollary to the Monroe Doctrine:

> All that this country desires is to see the neighboring countries
> stable, orderly, and prosperous. Any country whose people conduct
> themselves well can count upon our hearty friendship. If a nation
> shows that it knows how to act with reasonable efficiency and
> decency in social and political matters, if it keeps order and pays
> its obligations, it need fear no interference from the United States.
> Chronic wrongdoing, or an impotence which results in a general
> loosening of the ties of civilized society, may in America, as elsewhere,
> ultimately require intervention by some civilized nation, and in
> the Western Hemisphere the adherence of the United States to the
> Monroe Doctrine may force the United States, however reluctantly, in
> flagrant cases of such wrongdoing or impotence, to the exercise of an
> international police power.[63]

A series of relatively undistinguished functionaries passed through the role of governor of Puerto Rico in the immediate ensuing years, their chief recommendation often appearing to be their proximity to power in

Washington rather than their grasp of the complexities of Puerto Rico. Meanwhile, the island's internal politics continued to evolve. In February 1904, the Partido Federal became the Unión de Puerto Rico (UPR), formed by Luis Muñoz Rivera along with Rosendo Matienzo Cintrón, Antonio Rafael Barceló, Eduardo Georgetti, and José de Diego. The UPR would be the island's dominant political party for much of the next thirty years, and the newspaper *La Democracia* (also founded by Muñoz Rivera) effectively acted as a UPR publication.

Now in his fifties, Muñoz Rivera's political star appeared ascendant. In 1910, he ran for—and won—the office of resident commissioner as a candidate for the UPR, and began to serve in March 1911. It was in this capacity that he watched as the US Congress debated the adoption of legislation sponsored by Democratic Representative William Atkinson Jones of Virginia and Senator John Shafroth of Colorado that would reorganize the island's system of government, grant US citizenship to most Puerto Rican citizens, make its male population subject to the draft, and exempt Puerto Rican bonds from all federal, state, and local taxes. The bill would eventually be referred to as the Jones–Shafroth Act, after its two main sponsors. A subsequent, separate piece of legislation, the Merchant Marine Act of 1920—sponsored by Washington Republican senator Wesley Jones and also referred to as the Jones Act—mandated that all goods going to and from Puerto Rico be transported on ships constructed and flagged in the United States and owned and staffed solely by US citizens or, in the latter case, permanent residents.

It was in response to the earlier piece of legislation winding its way through Congress that Muñoz Rivera rose on May 5, 1916, and gave a long, impassioned speech that included the following words:

> On the eighteenth day of October 1898, when the flag of this great
> Republic was unfurled over the fortresses of San Juan, if anyone had
> said to my countrymen that the United States, the land of liberty, was

going to deny their right to form a government of the people, by the people, and for the people of Puerto Rico, my countrymen would have refused to believe such a prophecy, considering it sheer madness.[64]

Pointing out that, under the late Spanish colonial system, Puerto Ricans were due to enjoy more rights than they enjoyed under the Foraker Act passed sixteen years earlier, he went on to state:

> In Puerto Rico no blood will be shed. . . . Its narrow confines never permitted and never will permit armed resistance. For this very reason Puerto Rico is a field of experiment unique on the globe. And if Spain, the reactionary monarchy, gave Puerto Rico the home rule which she was enjoying in 1898, what should the United States, the progressive Republic, grant her?

Calling the bill "meager and conservative," Muñoz Rivera nevertheless concluded that it was "a step in the right direction" and "a reform paving the way for other more acceptable and satisfactory which shall come a little later" and urged its adoption.

Adopted it would indeed be, but Don Luis would not live to see its impact. Returning to Puerto Rico after the exhausting debate, he grew gravely ill from a gallbladder infection. After spending his entire adult life advocating on behalf of the island, on November 15, 1916, Luis Muñoz Rivera died. There was an outpouring of grief both in the capital and in his hometown of Barranquitas, where he was buried among crowds of jíbaros from the mountains and young girls dressed all in white as a band played *La Borinqueña*.[65]

In July 1921, the governorship passed to Emmet Montgomery Reily. A Missouri-born politician and journalist who had drifted through Texas and his home state, Reily was selected for the job chiefly due to his support for

Republican president Warren G. Harding. In his inauguration speech, Reily declared that there was "no room on this island for any flag other than the stars and stripes," and in letters home to Harding he mocked the Puerto Ricans as "children" and revealed an obsession with the role of "negroes" on the island.[66] Perhaps unsurprisingly, the jingoistic Reily proved an extremely unpopular choice and, as it happened, his tenure coincided with the return to Puerto Rico of one of the most extraordinary figures the island has ever produced.

One of those who had watched the US troops fan out over Puerto Rico more than two decades earlier was the seven-year-old illegitimate son of a Basque merchant and a mixed-race woman in Ponce. His name was Pedro Albizu Campos. A brilliant student, he was awarded a scholarship to the University of Vermont, where he studied chemistry, before transferring to continue his studies at Harvard University. He volunteered and served as a second lieutenant in the Army Reserve during World War I, and his exposure to racism both in the US South and in the military itself marked him deeply. After the war, he would return to Harvard and graduate from law school there in 1921. While at Harvard he met and married a Peruvian biochemist, Laura Meneses. Though he could have availed himself of any number of tempting job offers, he returned to Ponce to act as a lawyer for the poor and to pursue the cause that would be his true life's calling: independence for Puerto Rico.[67]

In 1922, the Supreme Court's decision in *Balzac v. Porto Rico* specified that, although the Jones Act had granted US citizenship to citizens of the island, it did not have full political status as a state and thus certain provisions of the US Constitution did not apply there. The decision as to what those provisions were was left to the US Congress.[68] That September, UPR dissidents José Coll y Cuchí and José S. Alegría founded the Partido Nacionalista de Puerto Rico (PNPR) to push for Puerto Rican independence. Two years later they were joined by thirty-three-year-old Albizu Campos, who became the PNPR's vice president. Clashes between Coll y Cuchí and Albizu Campos over the latter's more confrontational approach to the Americans would eventually result in the former's departure from the party to return to the UPR fold, and the election of the latter as PNPR president in May 1930. Albizu Campos had spent much of the previous three years traveling around Latin America, inveighing against the United States' authority over Puerto Rico, and stirring audiences to support Puerto Rican independence.[69] From the start, the PNPR's radicalism was fairly apparent and, to some, the PNPR's paramilitary group, *los cadetes de la republica*, suggested a rather spooky flirtation with tropical fascism, clad as they were in black shirts that called to mind the supporters of Italy's dictator Benito Mussolini.[70]

The situation was somewhat ameliorated when, from September 1929 to January 1932, the position of governor was held by Theodore "Ted" Roosevelt III, the eldest son of Theodore Roosevelt. As had his father and cousin Franklin Delano Roosevelt before him, Roosevelt had previously served as assistant secretary of the Navy, and his tenure marked something of an apogee of the United States' colonial relationship with the island (the year he arrived, Puerto Rico's legislature also granted women who could read and write the right to vote, a franchise that would be extended to all women six years later). Taking the trouble to actually become reasonably proficient in Spanish, Roosevelt traveled around the island and was soon referred to as *el Jíbaro de La Fortaleza* (the Hillbilly of the Governor's Mansion). Roosevelt also named the mycologist Carlos E. Chardón as Chancellor of the Universidad de Puerto Rico, the first Puerto Rican to hold that position.

After Roosevelt finished his term (he would die in France shortly after taking part in the Normandy landings during World War II a decade later), a trio of acting governors assumed control until, in February 1934, Blanton Winship, a career military man who had fought in both the Spanish-American War and World War I and appeared to view wartime politics and civilian politics through much the same unrelenting lens, was appointed to the position by President Franklin D. Roosevelt.

By this point, the yawning inequalities of the Puerto Rican system were hard to ignore. Historians noted that "in twenty years, the island was transformed from a largely agricultural district into an export-oriented manufacturing platform with decaying agricultural activity."[71] By 1930, US and Canadian banking interests were thought to control half the capital on the island.[72] Around 95 percent of Puerto Rico's external trade was with the United States,[73] and the island provided around 15 percent of the raw sugar consumed on the US market.[74] Between 1930 and 1933, per capita income fell by about 30 percent,[75] and San Juan received half of all internal migrants in Puerto Rico between 1935 and 1940.[76]

But there was an even darker side to the colonial relationship. Beginning in the 1930s, thousands of Puerto Rican women were sterilized, often without being informed about the permanent nature of the procedure and with no other method of contraception being offered. It was a phenomenon that grew even more severe after the 1937 passage of Law 116, a eugenics measure that argued, in the main, that such a program would "catalyze economic growth," and that too many Puerto Rican babies would have a negative impact on the island's economic prospects. The procedure became so commonplace it was known simply as *la operacion*. By 1965, a survey would find that nearly one-third of all Puerto Rican mothers ages twenty to forty-nine were sterilized.[77] One of the great advocates against the practice, Dr. Helen Rodríguez Trías, was also a longtime independence activist, and pointedly observed that

> sterilization has been pushed . . . as a way of population control.
> And there is a difference between population control and birth control.
> Birth control exists as an individual right. It's something that should be
> built into health programming . . . Population control is really a social
> policy that's instituted with the thought in mind that there's some
> people who should not have children or should have very
> few children.[78]

The catalyst for a change in the island's fortunes could not have come in a more unlikely figure.

For much of the 1920s Luis Muñoz Marín, the son of Luis Muñoz Rivera, had lived a wildly bohemian poet's life, shuttling around the northeastern United States and, especially, New York City's Greenwich Village—where he became friends with the famous eccentric Joe Gould—with occasional forays back to Puerto Rico. He was often only a tangential presence in the lives of his wife (Mississippi-born American writer Muna Lee, who he would eventually divorce) and two children.[79] Though he had been born at 152 Calle de la Fortaleza in Old San Juan in February 1889, a mere six months before the US invasion, he spoke flawless English as a result of his years being educated in New York and Washington, DC, during his father's various diplomatic missions. Gradually, however, the fate of the island to which his father had devoted his life began to interest him. In a searing 1929 op-ed for the *American Mercury*, Muñoz Marín described the island's economy, writing that "large absentee-owned sugar estates, the rapid curtailment of the planting of coffee—the natural crop of the independent farmer—and the concentration of the cigar manufacture into the hands of the American trust have combined to make Puerto Rico a land of beggars and millionaires."[80] In 1931, he returned to Puerto Rico for good.

Within a year, Muñoz Marín had been elected to the island's Senate as a member of the pro-independence Partido Liberal. One American diplomat who met him said that Muñoz Marín's political skills were equal to those of Franklin Delano Roosevelt and New York City mayor Fiorello LaGuardia.[81] A secret FBI report, on the other hand, characterized him as "a political opportunist supported by radical politicians who desire Puerto Rico's independence from the United States. . . . He has no moral character, he is absolutely irresponsible financially, but he is probably the most brilliant politician on the political horizon of Puerto Rico."[82] (Rumours of drug abuse—specifically opium—clung so strongly to Muñoz Marín that he felt the need to publicly deny them after his return.[83])

Opportunist or not, the Americans would soon need all the friends they could get on the island.

A series of strikes in 1933 and 1934 saw tens of thousands of workers, led by the tobacco industry, walk off their jobs.[84] The PNPR was heavily involved in the action.[85] In Guayama, on June 11, 1934, Albizu Campos spoke to six thousand striking sugarcane workers and their supporters.[86] The much-feared US-appointed police chief on the island at the time, Francis Riggs, was a man of considerable power and influence beyond what his title might have suggested. The heir to the fortune of the Riggs National Bank, then one of the largest banks in the United States, Riggs had previously served in another US colonial adventure in Nicaragua. According to one story told by the author Nelson Antonio Denis, only days after his triumphant speech in Guayama, Albizu Campos was invited by Riggs to lunch at the tony Escambrón Beach Club in San Juan, whereupon he offered Albizu Campos $150,000 in political "support"—a bribe—and eventually the governorship if he and the PNPR would cease backing the strike. As cordially as he could, Albizu Campos replied that Puerto Rico was not for sale and left.[87]

On October 24, 1935, four PNPR supporters and a bystander were killed at the Universidad de Puerto Rico in Río Piedras in what became known as the Río Piedras Massacre. Acrimony had been building over a move by some students to declare Albizu Campos, who had fiercely denounced Universidad de Puerto Rico chancellor Dr. Carlos E. Chardón as a tool of US imperialism, as persona non grata on the campus. As tensions built, the campus was flooded with armed police on the orders of Blanton Winship. Almost exactly four months to the day of the massacre, in February 1936, Francis Riggs was gunned down by nationalists Elías Beauchamp and Hiram Rosado in retaliation. Beauchamp and Rosado were arrested and summarily executed at a San Juan police station, with Beauchamp photographed saluting just before being cut down and reportedly shouting,

Disparen para que vean, como muere un hombre! (Go ahead and shoot, then you'll see how a man dies!) In its coverage of the pair's funeral processions—which were attended by thousands—the island's *El Imparcial* used Beauchamp's final words as its headline.[88]

In April 1936, Maryland Senator Millard Tydings, then-chairman of the Committee on Territories and Insular Affairs, introduced a bill that would grant Puerto Rico independence if voters opted for it in a plebiscite. Though Muñoz Marín, then a senator, has often been pilloried for opposing the bill, what is often left out is the fact that, economically speaking, the bill essentially left the island to fend for itself, imposing a 25 percent tariff on goods exported from Puerto Rico to the United States, a measure that would have left the local economy stone-dead. Tydings would offer up variations on the same legislation five more times in the ensuing years, though it would never be adopted.[89]

On July 27, 1936, Albizu Campos was convicted by a jury of ten Americans and two people of Puerto Rican descent (handpicked by the US attorney prosecuting the case) of conspiracy to overthrow the US government and sentenced to ten years in prison.[90]

On March 21, 1937—Palm Sunday—with their most charismatic leader sitting in prison, several hundred nationalists gathered to legally march in Ponce after having obtained a permit. Ordered to disperse by Ponce mayor José Tormos Diego and local Insular Police commander Guillermo Soldevilla (acting on direct orders from Winship), the participants refused to do so and, as a band played *La Borinqueña*, began to march. The police opened fire and then stormed into the crowd, gunning some down and beating others senseless. During the police riot, nineteen people were killed, including a seven-year-old girl and two of the policemen's own, and some two hundred were injured. One cadete de la republica, Bolívar Márquez, wrote *¡Viva la República, Abajo los asesinos!* (Long live the Republic, down with the murderers!) in his own blood as he lay dying. Though Insular

Police Chief Colonel Enrique de Orbeta oversaw a farcical attempt at a cover-up, the truth soon became known, not least of all because the killings had taken place in full view of hundreds of witnesses. No police officers were ever punished for the killings, but a subsequent joint investigation by Arthur Garfield Hays of the American Civil Liberties Union and several prominent Puerto Ricans concluded that the event was an unwarranted massacre. The killing became known henceforth as the Ponce Massacre, and became one of the signal events in the collective memory of the nationalists. They had tried to press their demands peacefully and had been met with bullets in response.[91]

Extraordinarily after such a bloodbath, Winship was not recalled, and on July 25, 1938, he held a bellicose military parade in Ponce, complete with US Air Force planes flying over the crowd. Nationalist Angel Esteban Antongiorgi opened fire on Winship in the reviewing stand, succeeding in killing a National Guard soldier before he himself perished in a hail of bullets. The Italian-American congressman Vito Marcantonio, who represented East Harlem and its large Puerto Rican population, would denounce on the floor of the US Congress what he charged were Winship's "tyrannical acts . . . in depriving the people of Puerto Rico of their civil rights, the corruption and rackets that existed and were made possible only by the indulgence of the governor and the extraordinary waste of the people's money."[92]

Finally, in May 1939, Roosevelt recalled Winship, who then became a lobbyist for the sugar industry, fighting an increase in Puerto Rico's paltry minimum wage on their behalf (he lost).[93]

As Blanton Winship left the governor's office in 1939 after forty-one years of US rule of the island, he and his predecessors left an outpost that was still largely an agricultural society. Seventy percent of the population lived in rural areas, where an average of 109 children out of every one thousand died in infancy, malnutrition was widespread, and average life expectancy was forty-six years.[94] By the early 1940s, thousands of Puerto Ricans came to the East Coast to work as farm laborers in the summer, and would often stay until they returned to the island for sugarcane harvesting season in the winter.[95]

Though often given short shrift in Anglophone accounts of the island, the first half of the twentieth century also saw a vibrant debate among Puerto Rican literary figures, academics, and other intellectuals about the nature of what it meant to be Puerto Rican and, by extension, the nature of the island's relationship with the United States. In 1934, Antonio S. Pedreira published *Insularismo*, which examined the state of Puerto Rican identity and culture in the aftermath of the US invasion. In 1935, Tomás Blanco, who studied medicine at Georgetown University before traveling throughout the United States and Europe, published *Prontuario Histórico de Puerto Rico*, an examination of the island's relationship with Spain before the US invasion. In 1937, Guayama native Luis Palés Matos published *Tuntún de pasa y grifería* (Drumbeats of Kinkiness and Blackness), a collection of poetry that in many ways marked the most piercing salvo of a genre of poetry that become known as Afro-Antillano. Palés Matos's background in Guayama—one of the key cities in the slave-based sugar economy that was abolished only a little more than two decades before he was born, and the location of Pedro Albizu Campos's rousing 1934 address—deeply informed his worldview.

Though nearly two decades younger than Pedreira, Blanco, and Palés Matos, another Puerto Rican writer came of age during the early days of US rule and, perhaps more than any other, would intensely bring the reality of the island's beauty and pain home to readers across the world through the force of her poetry. The writer, Julia de Burgos, born in Carolina, Puerto Rico, in 1914, was brought up on a farm and in conditions of such poverty that six of her siblings died before they reached adulthood. When she was fourteen, her family moved to Río Piedras, closer to the capital, where she graduated from the Universidad de Puerto Rico at nineteen with a teaching degree. At the height of US repression of the island's Nationalist political strain, a cause to which she became committed, de Burgos wrote her first poems and married Nationalist journalist Rubén Rodríguez Beauchamp. They lived in Naranjito, where the *cordillera central* begin climbing toward the island's geographic center, before moving to Old San Juan in 1936. In 1938, after having separated from her husband, she met the Dominican writer and political activist Juan Isidro Jimenes Grullón, a decade older than she and a veteran of a stint in the prisons of Dominican dictator Rafael Trujillo. The pair moved to New York and then to Havana, beginning a pattern of restless wandering that would continue for much of de Burgos's life, even after she left Jimenes Grullón in 1942.[96] Somehow, though it all, she was was always writing, writing homages to Pedro Albizu Campos and Cuban independence hero José Martí, penning soaring verse such as that contained in *Río Grande de Loíza,* her tribute to the river she had known in her youth, and writing poems of deep personal despair like *Poemas para las lágrimas* (Poem for Tears).[97]

Though he would not fully convert publicly for some time, looking at the intractable codependent tangle of the United States in Puerto Rico, by the late 1930s Luis Muñoz Marín had become convinced that independence was an impossible dream. In July 1938, he and other dissidents in the pro-independence Partido Liberal formed a new political grouping, the Partido Popular Democrático (PPD), which would dominate the island's political life for the next three decades. As its symbol, the party chose the silhouette of a straw-hatted jíbaro to demonstrate its purported links with the common man. Though its slogan was *Pan, Tierra y Libertad* (Bread, Land, and Freedom), the party's goal would not be the island's independence, but rather economic development to lift its citizens out of poverty. Ahead of the November 1940 elections, the PPD, led by Muñoz Marín, campaigned tirelessly in the rural hinterlands of the island, promising curious jíbaros that a new day was coming if they would give the PPD a chance in power. In his closing speech before the vote, Muñoz Marín, carrying forward with the populist strain that had typified the campaign, proclaimed that a vote for the PPD would replace the time of "the managers," which saw the country adrift and bereft, with the time of "the people." It was a logical continuation of the "time of the patriots" brought forth by men like his father.[98] The people of Puerto Rico decided to give him that chance. The PPD swept the elections, and Muñoz Marín became the president of Puerto Rico's Senate.

The next few years would see a swirl of activity in the island's political landscape. A month before the vote that brought the PPD to power, the Nationality Act of 1940 expanded the US citizenship granted to most Puerto Ricans. The new law was a change from the *jus sanguinis* (blood right) that had been enacted through the Jones–Shafroth Act (meaning persons born in Puerto Rico were technically born outside the United States, but were US citizens if their parents were also born in Puerto Rico, or were born in the mainland US), to a *jus soli* (right of soil or birthright), meaning thereafter all born in Puerto Rico would automatically acquire US citizenship (regardless of where their parents were born).[99] In September 1946, the PPD's Jesús T. Piñero became the first Puerto Rican to serve as the US-appointed governor of the island. Muñoz Marín had a savvy eye for sussing out political talent, and in 1947, the feminist activist Felisa Rincón de Gautier, who would become widely referred to as *Doña Fela*, became mayor of San Juan on the PPD's ticket. The first woman to be elected as the mayor of a capital city in the Americas, she would hold the office for the party for the next twenty-two years.

The same year Doña Fela ascended to the mayorship, an industrial initiatives act signaled the starting gun of what became known as Operation Bootstrap, an aggressive program of industrialization that nevertheless also saw significant agrarian reform focused on the sugar industry. What followed was a rapid depopulation of the impoverished countryside, with the more than two hundred thousand workers who toiled in agriculture at Operation Bootstrap's outset falling to 124,000 a little over a decade later.[100] Muñoz Marín and the PPD promoted an extremely statist model of development, turning the wheel of the island's economic engine toward an urban, export-oriented model. To this end, the Industrial Incentives Act of May 1947 eliminated the Puerto Rican corporate tax entirely.[101]

As is often the case, the more power the PPD accumulated, the more it seemed to crave. In June 1948, the infamous Law 53, better known as the *Ley de la Mordaza* (Gag Law) was signed into law by Piñero after being passed by the Puerto Rican Senate where Muñoz Marín served as president.[102] The law made it a felony to "encourage, advocate, advise or preach, voluntarily or knowingly, the need, desirability or convenience of overthrowing, destroying or paralyzing" the island's government as well as to "print, publish, edit, circulate, sell, distribute or publicly display" any material advocating that intention.[103] The law was, in many ways, a cover for Luis Muñoz Marín to pressure the Nationalists through more aggressive means. In that November's elections, the first ever in which the island's governor would be directly elected by the voters, Muñoz Marín was elected to the island's most powerful office with 61.2 percent of the vote. He entered the governor's mansion, La Fortaleza, in January 1949. Blocks away in his own home in Old San Juan, Pedro Albizu Campos, politically disempowered but not without weapons, bided his time and waited for the right moment to act.

That moment came on October 28, 1950, heralded with a wild jailbreak at the Río Piedras State Penitentiary, a forbidding neo-Moorish structure just south of San Juan popularly known as *El Oso Blanco* (the White Bear), where over one hundred prisoners escaped. In the aftermath, police raided the home of Nationalist Melitón Muñiz Santos in Ponce and found a fearsome array of weapons.[104] In Peñuelas, to the west of the city, six police officers were wounded and three Nationalists were killed in a shootout. In Jayuya, the Nationalist Blanca Canales lead nearly three dozen other Nationalists in an assault on the police station and other government buildings. The government responded by sending a P-47 Thunderbolt fighter aircraft to bomb and machine gun the town and then hundreds of National Guard troops to occupy it.[105] Nationalists in Utuado tried to overwhelm the police station but were repulsed by heavy fire. Four captured Nationalists were subsequently summarily executed in an alley near the town's police station (five others who were also shot survived). Like Jayuya, Utuado was also bombed from the air.[106] In a suicidal raid against the governor's mansion, La Fortaleza—with Muñoz Marín inside—four Nationalists were killed.[107] Elsewhere in San Juan, a single barber—PNPR sympathizer Vidal Santiago Díaz, who ran the Salón Boricua, which Albizu Campos often used as a meeting place—exchanged gunfire with security forces for several hours before being overwhelmed, wounded, and arrested.

But more was to come. On November 1, two Nationalists, Oscar Collazo and Griselio Torresola—who both hailed from Jayuya, which had been bombed only hours before—attacked Blair House in Washington, DC, where President Harry Truman was staying while the White House was undergoing renovations. After a wild gunfight, Torresola was killed, as was White House policeman Leslie W. Coffelt. Collazo, though gravely wounded, survived, and was convicted and sentenced to death in 1952. Truman commuted his sentence to life imprisonment a week before his scheduled execution. (In September 1979, President Jimmy Carter commuted Collazo's sentence to time served and he was freed, returning to Puerto Rico.) Albizu Campos himself was arrested at his home in Old San Juan after a gun battle with National Guard and police elements.

After the revolt, Muñoz Marín declared an island-wide state of emergency, something he'd previously been hesitant to do. Three thousand people would be arrested; a number of them, like Albizu Campos, were held in Cárcel La Princesa, the sprawling Spanish-era prison in Old San Juan dating from 1837. Its stifling, fetid cells overflowed with Nationalist prisoners, including the poet and essayist Francisco Matos Paoli, who served as the PNPR's secretary general.[108]

Albizu Campos would be sentenced to life in prison in August 1951 for his role in the uprising. During his time in prison, he would complain of "brilliant lights" penetrating his cell and was found by doctors to have unexplained burn marks on his body. His appendages swelled grotesquely. The few prisoners who shared his cell made similar complaints. He covered himself in wet towels to try and ward off the effects of whatever was bedeviling him, and as a result prison guards mockingly called him *El Rey de las Toallas* (The King of the Towels). Whether prison authorities were conducting some sort of experiments on him has never been definitely proven, although, at the time, such experiments were hardly unheard-of—in locales such as the Stateville Penitentiary in Illinois, for example, patients were intentionally infected with malaria for three decades so doctors could experiment with treatments of the disease.

3

IN A FREE STATE (OF SORTS)

IN ITS FINAL SUICIDAL LUNGE, PUERTO RICO'S INDEPENDENCE movement had been all but vanquished. In a March 1952 referendum, the island's voters were asked to affirm or reject a new constitution, one that would characterize the island as an Estado Libre Asociado (Freely Associated State or, more commonly, Commonwealth) of the United States. The option of independence was not on the ballot, and 81.9 percent of voters approved the new constitution. In November 1953, the United Nations removed Puerto Rico from its list of countries under colonial rule.

As their political fortunes evaporated, the Nationalists had one last card to play. In March 1954, four Nationalists—Rafael Cancel Miranda, Andres Figueroa Cordero, Irvin Flores, and Lolita Lebrón—attacked the US House of Representatives in Washington, DC. Shouting, *¡Viva Puerto Rico libre!* (Long live free Puerto Rico!) and unfurling a Puerto Rican flag, they used automatic pistols to rain bullets on the in-session chamber. Miraculously, no one was killed, though five lawmakers were seriously wounded.[109] Pedro Albizu Campos, who had been released conditionally by

Muñoz Marín only a few months earlier, was quickly rearrested. In March 1956, Albizu Campos had a stroke and, supporters charged, was denied medical attention for two days.[110] He would finally be released from prison in November 1964, a shadow of his former self, and died five months later.

Along with the near-total downfall of Puerto Rico's radical independence movement came another passing, this one perhaps even sadder—the death of the poet whose verse seemed to embody so many of the island's struggles, as well as its beauty and pain: Julia de Burgos.

After leaving Cuba in 1942 following the breakup of her relationship with Juan Isidro Jimenes Grullón, de Burgos had moved back to New York City. There, following the trajectory of so many from the island before her, she wrote for a Spanish-language weekly, and also began a relationship with a musician from Vieques named Armando Marín, whom she eventually married. A brief move to the suburbs of Washington, DC, ended in failure, and her FBI file, like those of so many partial to the independence cause before her, continued to grow. When her marriage collapsed she moved back to New York, and as she worked a series of blue-collar jobs, alcoholism and despair gradually overtook her.[111] On July 5, 1953, de Burgos was found unconscious on the sidewalk by two policemen in East Harlem and rushed to a hospital. She died of pneumonia at the age of thirty-nine and was buried in the potter's field on Hart Island in the Bronx. [112] It wasn't until the following month that her death was discovered by those who knew her and a committee, led by the great educator Margot Arce de Vázquez, was able to raise funds to repatriate her body to the island and give her a proper burial. In one of de Burgos's last poems, "Farewell from Welfare Island," she wrote, even as ill health and despondency took hold of her, of refusing to be forgotten:

> It has to come from here,
> right this instance,
> my cry into the world.

After a lifetime of struggle, Julia de Burgos was at peace. In Puerto Rico, the battles would go on.

In the mid-1950s, after more than fifty years of American rule, Puerto Rico was connected more deeply than ever to the United States, and the next two decades would see profound changes across the island.

Agriculture declined sharply after the advent of Operation Bootstrap with its focus on industrialization.[113] In 1956, the income generated by manufacturing outstripped that generated by agriculture for the first time.[114] Between 1953 and 1963, salaries in manufacturing on the island more than doubled.[115] As industrialization led to internal migration, San Juan and other cities saw the growth of shantytowns, such as those along the Caño Martín Peña (Martín Peña Channel), which runs from the Bahía de San Juan in the west to a pair of lagoons—San José and Los Corozos—in the east. The Los Peloteros shantytown was home to nearly seventeen thousand people who lived there despite its lack of a sewage system. More than 421 similar communities existed around the island by 1959.[116] Perhaps the most iconic was La Perla, just beneath the walls of Old San Juan along the Caribbean Sea. First settled at the tail end of the nineteenth century on the site of what was then a slaughterhouse, La Perla was initially home to many descendants of former slaves and poor arrivals from the countryside. Over the years, the neighborhood's distinctive homes—at first mere wooden shacks that were over time replaced by mainly concrete structures painted ebullient colors—became one of the more recognizable images of the island.[117] For those in less stark circumstances, preplanned residential developments, similar to what one would find in suburbs in the US mainland, sprouted up around cities like San Juan, Ponce, and Mayagüez. Family income on the island rose from $660 a year in 1940 to $3,818 a year in 1966.[118] Between 1940 and 1970, illiteracy would drop from 34 percent to 10.8 percent.[119]

During the 1950s, though the number of jobs on the island fell by some sixty thousand, the escape valve provided by easy migration to the United States proved enticing, and tens of thousands of Puerto Ricans left the island for better-paying jobs on the mainland, preventing the widespread social unrest that occurred elsewhere in Latin America.[120] According to the US census, by 1960 nearly 900,000 people of Puerto Rican descent were living in the United States, with almost 70 percent having been born in Puerto Rico.[121]

After the events of the 1950s, independence advocates, electorally minded and otherwise, had a hard path to trod. But while Muñoz Marín's gambit proved successful on many fronts, it was met with a backlash from those Puerto Ricans who were not at all sure if this was the direction they wanted their beloved island to go in.

The Partido Independentista Puertorriqueño (PIP) had been founded in October 1946 by the attorney Gilberto Concepción de Gracia and the poet Fernando Milán Suárez. It was a substantial political force, coming in second in the November 1952 legislative elections, just behind Muñoz Marín's PPD. Gilberto Concepción de Gracia himself became a senator, a post he would hold until 1960. The second half of the 1950s, though, saw the independence movement beset by internal political squabbles. The Partido Socialista, which thirty years earlier was pulling 25 percent of the vote, would collapse and many members would gravitate to the PPD. By 1959, one of the most forceful proponents of independence, Juan Mari Brás, would leave the PIP to form the more militant Movimiento Pro-Independencia (MPI) with Loida Figueroa Mercado. Along with the labor activist and author César Andreu Iglesias, Mari Brás launched the newsweekly *Claridad* as the voice of the Puerto Rican independence movement that same year.

It would be wrong to conclude that all of the Puerto Rican independence movement's wounds were self-inflicted, though. With the FBI targeting Puerto Rican independence activists in the United States since the mid-1950s under its Counter Intelligence Program (better known by its portmanteau COINTELPRO), the body's director, J. Edgar Hoover, instructed agents to procure information "concerning their weaknesses, morals, criminal records, spouses, children, family life, educational qualifications and personal activities" in an effort "to disrupt their activities and compromise their effectiveness."[122] Puerto Rican police dossiers, known as *carpetas*, did much the same work.[123] The carpetas covering the activities of Mari Brás would eventually total nearly twenty thousand pages, the first written in 1947 and the last that is known in 1985. Mari Brás was stalked at meetings and rallies and even at the funeral of his father, and extensive lists were compiled of everyone he interacted with, from independentistas to trade unionists, feminists, environmentalists, and other activists of various kinds. The files represented, the Puerto Rican academic Javier Colón Morera noted, the "bureaucratization of institutional repression."[124]

By this point, a not-entirely-flattering image of Puerto Ricans had also taken hold in the minds of some on the mainland, reinforced in part by the 1957 Leonard Bernstein and Stephen Sondheim musical *West Side Story* (later made into an Oscar-winning 1961 film), with its refrains, "Always the hurricanes blowing / Always the population growing / And the money owing / And the babies crying / And the bullets flying."[125] In academia, one of the works most responsible for creating this stark image in the public mind was the book *La Vida: A Puerto Rican Family in the Culture of Poverty—San Juan and New York*, by the American anthropologist Oscar Lewis. Many Puerto Ricans and even other scholars, however, felt that Lewis's portrayal was unrealistic in its unrelenting grimness, finding "little of the hopelessness and apathy" among the poor that Lewis had, and noting that "even the poorest families aspire toward a better future for themselves and their children."[126]

In November 1961—seven months after the failure of the Bay of Pigs invasion—President John F. Kennedy held a state dinner for Puerto Rico's governor Luis Muñoz Marín at the White House, a rare honor during which the Spanish-Puerto Rican cellist Pablo Casals performed. The following month, Kennedy arrived in San Juan and was greeted by Muñoz Marín at the airport, where he also addressed reporters:

> It is a great experience to fly many hundreds of miles into the Atlantic Ocean, to come to an island and be greeted in Spanish. To come to an island which has an entirely different tradition and history. Which is made up of people of an entirely different cultural origin than the mainland of the United States, and still be able to feel that I am in my country as I was in Washington this morning.[127]

The American view of Cuba setting its sights on Puerto Rico and trying to foment unrest there was not as far-fetched as it may now sound. As early as 1950, while still a young law student, Fidel Castro had been publishing articles calling for Puerto Rican independence, and one of the first friends he made during his 1955 to 1956 exile from Cuba in Mexico City was Albizu Campos's wife, Laura Meneses, at which time her husband was still in prison.[128] By this point, though, after the mass arrests, firing squads, and exile that followed Cuba's 1959 revolution and Castro's subsequent self-reveal as dictator and a Marxist-Leninist, many Puerto Ricans took a rather more circumspect view of the independentistas and their radical visions. As the anthropologist Helen Icken Safa would write, much of the underclass on the island feared "that if Puerto Rico becomes independent, it will experience bloodshed and revolution such as have occurred in Cuba and the Dominican Republic."[129]

In 1964, after more than three decades of nonstop political battle and four terms as governor, Muñoz Marín announced at the PPD's 1964 convention that he would not seek another term, telling attendees:

You must continue to have confidence in yourselves. Only then will I know I have created a people of determination, with strength and with spirit. . . . I am not your strength. You are your own source of strength. Forward, forward. I am with you and I remain a part of you.[130]

Muñoz Marín's relations with his designated successor, Roberto Sánchez Vilella, who won the governorship on the PPD ticket the following year, were often frosty. A July 1967 referendum on the status of the island gave voters the choice between remaining a commonwealth, statehood, or independence, with 60.4 percent opting for the commonwealth option. Differing opinions on the approach to the referendum led pro-statehood forces to fracture and inspired the creation of the Partido Nuevo Progresista (PNP), which vowed to push for Puerto Rico's status as the fifty-first state.

Sánchez Vilella's administration was hobbled not only by frequent clashes with Muñoz Marín, but also by a complicated personal life that led him to divorce his first wife and remarry just before the 1968 gubernatorial election, which his political opponents used to incite the island's not-insubstantial number of conservative Catholic voters against him. In 1968, amid the political wrangling, in a move that would have significant future impact, the US Congress capped federal funding for Medicaid on the island in a way that was still envisioned to cover 50 percent of the island's expenses. However, as healthcare costs rose in the coming decades, the federal contribution would shrink to less than 18 percent of Medicaid expenses—while states, with their need assessed by per-person income, would have had their Medicare costs covered at a rate of 83 percent.[131]

By the late 1960s, the ossifying of PPD rule dovetailed with the current mood of worldwide revolutionary social and political movements. After the 1967 plebiscite, the PPD lost the governor's election for the first time in 1968. The office went to Luis A. Ferré, a Ponce industrialist and candidate of the pro-statehood PNP, which he had helped found only the previous year. Born in Puerto Rico to a family with Cuban and French roots, Ferré had studied at both the Massachusetts Institute of Technology and the New England Conservatory of Music (he was a skilled classical pianist), and during his years on the mainland said he became enamored with "the American way of democracy," a form that was conspicuously still lacking on the island of his birth.[132]

Perhaps every bit as impactful as Ferré's election, however, was the fact that after nearly two decades of relative calm, political divisions on the island, again largely revolving around the question of independence, spiraled into what became known as the *guerra chiquita* (little war), which pitted radical independentistas against the state, both local and national, and its security forces. At the center of the violence was a former salsa musician from the eastern coastal town of Naguabo, whose time in Fidel Castro's Cuba had instilled a belief that nonviolent struggles were useless and that any political pressure to divest Puerto Rico from its colonial relationship with the United States must be accompanied by a kind of armed propaganda of military action.[133] His name was Filiberto Ojeda Ríos.

In many ways, up until that point, the life of Ojeda Ríos had been an intermingling of strains familiar to the stories of many Puerto Ricans, though his precocious intelligence—he enrolled at the Universidad de Puerto Rico at fifteen—set him apart. For much of the 1950s, he drifted back and forth between the island and New York, where, as a multi-instrumentalist, he worked with various musical groups. He moved to Cuba in 1961, only two years after Fidel Castro had seized power, and there developed close links with the Dirección General de Inteligencia, the main state intelligence agency of the Cuban government. Upon his return to Puerto Rico, many in US law enforcement believed he was working as a Cuban spy.[134] In 1967, he formed his first armed group, the Movimiento Independentista Revolucionario Armado (MIRA), which had little impact before being crushed by the police. Ojeda Ríos would eventually move back to New York, where he set about organizing a group that would have a far greater—and more deadly—impact.[135] While Ojeda Ríos was shifting the focus of his armed propaganda campaign to the mainland, the independence movement on the island was going through its own transformation.

In 1971, the MPI of Juan Mari Brás became the Partido Socialista Puertorriqueño (PSP), continuing in the hard-left vein and drawing inspiration from the example of Fidel Castro's Cuba, after which the MPI was founded.[136] The previous year, Rubén Berríos, an attorney from Aibonito, had taken over the leadership of the more conventionally social-democratic PIP. Both parties would fare very poorly in the 1976 elections, and in successive elections thereafter. Berríos, however, would be elected to the Senate on three separate occasions.

As it happened, though, what are widely regarded as the first shots of the guerra chiquita were not fired by committed independentistas but by the Puerto Rican police. In March 1970, Antonia Martínez Lagares, a twenty-one-year-old student at the Universidad de Puerto Rico, was shot and killed by police trying to break up a protest against the presence of the Reserve Officers' Training Corps (ROTC) on campus. While yelling from a balcony at a policeman she saw beating a student, Martínez was shot in the head. No one was ever prosecuted for the crime.[137]

In 1970, 160 bombs or incendiary devices were found around the island.[138] Though the left-wing terrorism of the independentistas would garner far more media coverage, placing bombs would remain a favored modus operandi of Puerto Rico's right wing throughout the 1970s.[139] The car of the PSP's Mari Brás was bombed by right wingers in January 1969, and in an attempt to further factionalize the movement, the FBI sent not one but two letters to Puerto Rican media claiming to be from independence groups acting against "communists."[140] The offices of *Claridad* were bombed on average once a year for five years.[141] The noted political analyst Juan Manuel García Passalacqua characterized the situation as one where, "losing ground very rapidly, pro-independence groups are getting desperate. Noticing that, anti-independence forces are getting trigger happy."[142]

A large flashpoint of hostility, one that cut across political ideologies, was the US military presence on the coastal island of Vieques, a presence that had existed since 1941 and included the use of a live firing range. The US government claimed that the range was safe despite its proximity to populated and sensitive environmental areas, but military personnel who traversed the firing range there would sometimes start bleeding from the nose and vomiting and were subject to terrible headaches.

According to some former soldiers who served on the island—who later experienced severe health crises themselves—the US Army used napalm, depleted uranium, and Agent Orange on the island, the latter of which was used as a defoliant in the Vietnam War and which has conclusively been proven to have a link to cancer and other illnesses.[143] If you lived on Vieques, you were eight times more likely to die of cardiovascular disease than someone living anywhere else in Puerto Rico, and you were seven times more likely to die of diabetes. Although it was not widely known until years later, the cancer rate for residents of Vieques was also higher than it was for residents living anywhere else in the commonwealth.[144]

During a May 19, 1979, demonstration in Vieques, more than one hundred demonstrators—including priests, pastors, and attorneys—waded ashore onto the island's beach and were arrested by naval policemen. Several were sentenced to prison terms ranging from thirty days to six months.[145]

Among those arrested that day was Ángel Rodríguez Cristóbal, a thirty-three-year-old member of the small *Liga Socialista Puertorriqueña*. Six months later, he was found dead in his prison cell at the Federal Correctional Institution in Tallahassee, Florida. Prison officials claimed he had committed suicide by hanging, but few, if any, in the independence movement believed this when photos of the body showed a three-inch gash from the Rodríguez Cristóbal's right eyebrow to his cheek. At his funeral in the mountain town of Ciales, Liga Socialista's founder, Juan Antonio Corretjer, warned that "the sounds and odors of gunpowder will prevail until the Navy has been driven from Vieques and the US from Puerto Rico."[146]

In 1972, Ferré lost his reelection bid, and the PPD was back in power once more in the person of Rafael Hernández Colón, a US-educated attorney and university lecturer who had served as president of Puerto Rico's Senate since 1968. Many had thought that Ferré would cruise to reelection and the result, with Ferré losing to Hernández Colón by nearly one hundred thousand votes, was considered a stunning upset.[147] The pro-statehood movement would grow from the mid-1970s onward, with the PPD and PNP mimicking the two-party duopoly on the mainland United States.

The first half of the 1970s would mark difficult economic times for the island. From the late 1960s to the mid-1970s, as a global economic downturn was also sharply felt on the island, a series of often-violent labor clashes occurred, some of them linked to a new, more radical labor movement, the Movimiento Obrero Unido (MOU).[148] In January 1973, President Richard Nixon initiated a year-long freeze on federally funded housing projects, which hit the island's construction industry particularly hard and coincided with the overbuilding of luxury high-rise condominiums which then sat vacant.[149] By mid-decade, a Puerto Rican government committee recommended a limit on government spending and pay increases, restricting wages and increasing tax revenue by raising land and real property taxes and taxes on durable consumer and luxury goods. The Hernández Colón administration quickly froze government wages thereafter.[150] By March 1976, Puerto Rico's official unemployment rate was 19.2 percent, but many thought the true rate was closer to 30 percent.[151] An incident in June 1976, where Hernández Colón had to scale a fence, cutting his hand in the process, and run through mud in order to be on time to greet President Gerald Ford at San Juan's airport (his limousine had a flat tire and got stuck in traffic), only to hear Ford deliver bland anti-Cuban platitudes, seemed for some to symbolize the island's servile relationship with the United States.[152]

Though it never posed any serious military threat to security forces on the island, even as Ford spoke the guerra chiquita churned on, and it now reached deep into the American mainland.

In the United States, Filiberto Ojeda Ríos helped to found the Fuerzas Armadas de Liberación Nacional (FALN). The FALN, composed to a large degree of diaspora Puerto Ricans who had grown up in the United States, including Vietnam War veteran Oscar López Rivera, was an altogether more muscular—and deadly—outfit than MIRA had been.[153] It announced its existence with a December 1974 booby trap in an East Harlem basement that cost Puerto Rican NYPD officer Angel Poggi his right eye and sent nails into his neck. (Poggi survived, but was confined to desk duty thereafter.)[154]

On January 11, 1975, a bomb exploded at a restaurant frequented by Puerto Rican nationalists in Mayagüez, a block from where a PSP rally was underway, killing two and injuring eleven.[155] Two weeks later, a bomb tore through Fraunces Tavern, a Revolutionary War-era bar in Manhattan's financial district, killing four and injuring forty. In a phone call to the Associated Press, a caller claiming to be a member of the FALN took responsibility for the blast. A note in a nearby phonebooth, also purporting to be from the FALN, said that the group took "full responsibility for the especially detonated [sic] bomb that exploded today at Fraunces Tavern, with reactionary corporate executives inside" and said that the attack was in retaliation for the "CIA ordered bomb" in Mayagüez.[156]

Speaking to the US Senate Subcommittee to Investigate the Administration of the Internal Security Act in July 1975, one "Francisco Martinez," a "consultant and researcher for several private interests in Puerto Rico industrial companies in the field of labor relations," who "for reasons of personal security" testified "under an assumed name," told the senators that Juan Mari Brás's PSP was "not only a subversive organization, but an active instrument of a foreign government [i.e. Cuba] dedicated to the destruction of democratic principles on which the government of the Commonwealth of Puerto Rico is based. . . . The Party's relations with Cuba are so close that it has a permanent delegation and offices in Havana."[157] The following month, Fidel Castro held a "Puerto Rican Solidarity Conference" in Havana.[158]

In January 1977, the PNP again returned to La Fortaleza; this time in the person of Carlos Romero Barceló, who had served as San Juan's mayor for nearly a decade previously. One of the PNP's most fervent evangelists for what he viewed as the benefits of further deepening the relationship with the United States, he had authored a pamphlet titled *La estadidad es para los pobres* (Statehood is for the Poor), whose title more or less summed up his argument. Writing in *Foreign Affairs*, Romero Barceló argued that the island's commonwealth status was a "myth" and that "statehood for Puerto Rico would constitute a boon for the nation, as well as for the island" and would enable "political equality within a framework which will permit our island and our nation to prosper together."[159] In the election that brought Romero Barceló to office, the independence vote had improved—the PIP president Rubén Berríos received 83,037 votes, a gain of thirteen thousand over the PIP's 1972 candidate—but was still paltry by comparison. Romero Barceló received 703,968 votes.[160]

Because of its one-sided dependent relationship with the mainland, Puerto Rico had remained in a kind of economic purgatory, never falling into the depths of want experienced by many other Latin American nations, yet never achieving the affluence and diversified economy of the rest of the United States. In his 1976 novel *La Guaracha del Macho Camacho* (Macho Camacho's Beat), it was no mistake that the Puerto Rican author Luis Rafael Sánchez used one of San Juan's apocalyptic traffic jams as a metaphor for an island stuck in place, unable to go backward or forward.

But despite its struggles, at home and on the mainland, Puerto Rico's luminous culture continued to flourish. Drawing from a mélange of influences that included the island's Afro-descended *bomba* music as well as the stylings of such figures as the singer Daniel Santos, the Cuban-American musician Machito, and the New York-born timbale player Tito Puente, the salsa genre exploded onto the Latin music scene by the 1960s. It was helped in no small part by the advent of Fania Records, a label founded in 1964 by Dominican band leader Johnny Pacheco and Italian-American music promoter Jerry Masucci. By the early 1970s, the label's "super group," the Fania All-Stars, was playing sold-out shows in New York City's Yankee Stadium, while the imprint also brought work by such pivotal acts as the Nuyorican trombonist Willie Colón and the Ponce-born singer Héctor Lavoe to a wide audience. Other groups like the salsa "orchestra" El Gran Combo recorded for other labels, also promoting the genre. Another singer, Ismael Rivera, had a career as a beloved exponent of the genre, singing socially conscious salsa tracks such as "Las Caras Lindas" (The Beautiful Faces), which celebrated blackness with lines like *Las caras lindas de mi gente negra / son un desfile de melaza en flor* (The beautiful faces of my black people / they are a parade of molasses in bloom), and the song "La Perla," which praised the often-stigmatized residents of the impoverished neighborhood that fronted the Caribbean beneath Old San Juan as "noble citizens" who "earn their bread with sweat" and whose "youth dream of tomorrow."

In New York City, the Nuyorican experience synthesized into a gripping new genre of poetry as purveyed by authors such as Miguel Algarín, Pedro Pietri, Sandra María Esteves, and Jesús Papoleto Meléndez. Eventually centered around what became known as the Nuyorican Poets Cafe on East 6th Street in the East Village (in 1980 they would move to a larger building on East 3rd Street), in many ways the foundation for this flowering had been laid by those who came before, such as Julia de Burgos and the playwright René Marqués, whose most famous work, *La Carreta*, had its premiere in Manhattan in 1954. It was an aesthetic that was simultaneously informed by a freewheeling Beat Generation–style sensibility, wedded to New York, and vibrantly Puerto Rican, and was perhaps best summed up in a poem by the doomed Nuyorican poet Miguel Piñero:

I don't wanna be buried in Puerto Rico
I don't wanna rest in long island cemetery
I wanna be near the stabbing shooting
gambling fighting & unnatural dying
& new birth crying
So please when I die . . .
don't take me far away
keep me near by
take my ashes and scatter them thru out
the Lower East Side . . . [161]

From somewhere, one would like to think, Julia de Burgos looked down and smiled.

But the island itself continued to smolder.

On July 4, 1978, two independence supporters, Pablo Marcano García and Nydia Esther Cuevas, kidnapped Chilean consul Ramón González Ruíz and another man, holding them hostage in a bank as US independence festivities went on blocks away. The pair demanded the release of Lolita Lebrón, Rafael Cancel Miranda, and Irvin Flores Rodríguez, all imprisoned since the 1954 attack on the US House of Representatives, and Oscar Collazo, in prison since the 1950 attempt to kill President Harry Truman. They finally surrendered to police after a seventeen-hour standoff, with Cuevas, upon being asked her age, replying, "I am as old as Lolita has been in prison."[162] (She was twenty-four.)

A series of articles in *El Nuevo Día* had quoted unnamed police sources and warned about upcoming independista violence for the summer of 1978,[163] and an incident that occurred that same month gave some indication of the lengths to which *la uniformada*, as the island's police were often called, were willing to go to confront what they viewed as a terrorist threat.

Carlos Enrique Soto Arriví was the son of Pedro Juan Soto, a well-known and respected author and university professor, and had grown up partially in Spain and France while his parents pursued doctoral degrees. Arnaldo Darío Rosado Torres was the studious, troubled son of an army veteran father, with whom he had stayed behind on the island when his mother and little brother moved to Brooklyn, not wanting to leave the elder Rosado "all alone."[164] Alejandro González Malavé was a Puerto Rican policeman who had begun infiltrating independence organizations while still in high school and had become a full-fledged undercover agent in March 1977.[165] Soto Arriví and Rosado Torres were members of a tiny would-be revolutionary group calling itself the Movimiento Revolucionario Armado, into whose midst González Malavé infiltrated, bringing its total membership to five. Among the group's "actions" were the theft of walkie-talkies and the firing of a shot, which hit no one, at the Universidad de Puerto Rico security offices.[166]

On July 25, 1978—the eightieth anniversary of the US invasion—the trio decided to make a statement by disabling a pair of radio transmitters on Cerro Maravilla, the island's fourth-highest peak, which rose to a height of some 3,953 feet as it vaulted out of the cordillera central on the border between Ponce and Jayuya. They carjacked a Ponce cab driver as Gonzales Malavé drove them into a trap. According to the account of the kidnapped driver, sixty-five-year-old Julio Ortiz Molina, Soto Arriví and Rosado Torres were executed by police and then Ortiz Molina was beaten to guarantee his silence. Gonzalez Malavé was wounded by shrapnel splintering off the car.[167] An April 1980 Department of Justice investigation concluded there was "no evidence that contradicted the police officers' official statements,"[168] but during a second round of investigations, Miguel Cartagena Flores, a detective in the Intelligence Division of the Puerto Rico Police Department, told investigators that Rosado Torres and Soto Arriví had been shot while "on their knees" and that Ángel Pérez Casillas, then commander of the intelligence division, had told officers that "these terrorists should not come down alive."[169] A decade after the killings on Cerro Maravilla, Pérez Casillas would be acquitted of the deaths while another policeman, Raphael Moreno, would be found guilty of second-degree murder. (Pérez Casillas and Moreno had been convicted of perjuring themselves before a Puerto Rican senate committee five years earlier).[170] Eventually, ten officers would be convicted for their roles in the killings and subsequent cover-up, with two also convicted of second-degree murder.[171]

González Malavé never spent a day in prison. Two months after he had been acquitted, he pulled into the driveway of his home in Bayamón. From two different directions a team of assassins approached him and executed him with three shotgun blasts, slightly injuring his mother in the process. A few hours later, the Organización de Voluntarios por la Revolución Puertorriqueña (OVRP) called the media to claim responsibility for the murder and announce that they would hunt down and kill "one by one" all the policemen involved in the Cerro Maravilla operation.[172]

On the twenty-eighth anniversary of the Jayuya Uprising (October 30, 1978), a communiqué was released by a group calling itself the Ejército Popular Boricua (EPB); it would later become known as Los Macheteros (The Machete Wielders). Formed two years earlier by Filiberto Ojeda Ríos and Juan Enrique Segarra-Palmer out of the ashes of the FALN, the group's missive, consciously or not, appeared to allude to the great gulf between its revolutionary fervor and the majority of the island's citizens, who had not rushed to align themselves with the EPB's cause. Beginning with a more or less pro forma vow to "make war against the invading Yankee and their representatives," the press release went on to threaten that the group was "willing to take this fight to the final consequences" and "would also judge and execute those who by their attitudes put at stake the security and development of the liberation struggle of our people."[173]

As if to prove these were not idle threats, on the morning of December 3, 1979, just before 7:00 a.m., gunmen leapt from a van and attacked a bus full of Navy personnel heading to the US Naval Base at Sabana Seca, killing two sailors and injuring ten, all of whom were unarmed. It was the first fatal attack on US military personnel on the island since 1970.[174] Along with the OVRP and the Fuerzas Armadas de Resistencia Popular (FARP), Los Macheteros claimed responsibility for the Sabana Seca attack, mentioning what it charged was the "murder" of Vieques protester Ángel Rodríguez Cristóbal and the Cerro Maravilla killings, and warning that "the blood of Puerto Rican martyrs and patriots will be mingled with the blood of the imperialists [and] the armed forces of the Yankee occupation will be the target of patriotic fire."[175] Despite the violence, Romero Barceló was reelected in 1980, defeating the PPD's Rafael Hernández Colón in a razor-thin vote whose recount dragged on for months and led to surreal scenes of Santeria sacrifices of chickens and invocations amid clouds of incense outside the building where the paper ballots were being counted.[176]

When Romero Barceló returned to office, the island was facing increasing economic pressure. Less than two years later, the US Congress would eliminate Puerto Rico's access to the Supplemental Nutrition Assistance Program (SNAP), more commonly referred to as "food stamps," in favor of what it dubbed the Nutrition Assistance Program for Puerto Rico. Known on the island as the Programa de Asistencia Nutricional, or colloquially as *cupones* (coupons), this block grant gave the island's government more flexibility but reduced the federal contribution.[177] Around the same time, J. Peter Grace, the head of a presidential panel called the Private Sector Survey on Cost Control, which recommended cuts in government operating costs, described SNAP as "basically a Puerto Rican program."[178]

On January 13, 1981, Los Macheteros blew up eight A-7 Corsair and F-104 Starfighter jets at Muñiz Air National Guard Base near the end of the main runway at San Juan's international airport. No one was injured, but damage was estimated at $45 million.[179] Following the attack, Los Macheteros released a communiqué claiming responsibility for the operation, which was named *Pitirre II* after a Puerto Rican songbird. Mentioning the murders of trade union leader Juan Rafael Caballero and Adolfina Villanueva Osorio, as well as the Cerro Maravilla killings, the group assailed the "colonial governor" Romero Barceló, who they said "progressively becomes more repressive and dictatorial against broad sectors of our people." The group reiterated what it said was its intention "to build a free, independent and neutral homeland without military service in a murderous foreign army and without Yankee military bases that expose our people to nuclear extermination."[180]

In November 1980, a squatter community, largely made up of those unemployed or underemployed and unable to pay rent, had sprung up near Canóvanas, east of San Juan. The community called itself *Villa Sin Miedo* (Town without Fear), and over the next two years, around 250 families would settle there.[181] The squatters were marginalized and harassed by the government and the police, and one of the few groups that did act, albeit violently, in their defense was Los Macheteros, who in November 1981 placed a bomb that knocked out electricity to twenty thousand customers in wealthy areas of San Juan to protest the refusal by the Puerto Rico Electric Power Authority (PREPA) to supply the village with power.[182] By May 1982, the government had had enough and brutally evicted the community, burning their homes and clothing in a violent conflagration in which a policeman was killed (authorities said they had seized a machine gun, five pistols, and a dagger in the raid).

Around two hundred Villa San Miedo residents occupied the lobby of the capitol building in San Juan, wailing to anyone who would listen that if they left they would "have nothing."[183] Los Macheteros responded to the eviction by placing several bombs in the luxurious Marbella del Caribe Oeste condominium, apparently under the mistaken impression that Secretary of Housing Jorge Pierluisi lived there. Two of the bombs went off, destroying a transformer and a trash depot, but there were no injuries.[184]

In September 1983, Los Macheteros made the headlines yet again when Víctor Gerena, a twenty-five-year-old who had thus far led a notably undistinguished life, tied up two employees at gunpoint and then robbed $7.2 million from the Wells Fargo depot in West Hartford, Connecticut, on the group's behalf, the largest cash robbery in US history up to that that time.[185] Gerena fled south to Mexico City, where a forged set of Argentine identity papers and a passport were hand-delivered to him by no less a personage than José Antonio Arbesú, who would go on to serve as the chief of the Cuban Interests Section in Washington, DC, from 1989 to 1992. Gerena then boarded a commercial flight to Havana, with over $2 million from the robbery flying with him in a Cuban diplomatic pouch.[186] Los Macheteros subsequently released a statement claiming responsibility for the robbery and said they had been planning it for nearly two years.[187] Ojeda Ríos would be arrested in August 1985 along with eleven other people in connection with the theft. Ojeda Ríos's indictment said he had been told by a representative of the Castro dictatorship that part of the money "remained in the custody and care of the Cuban government."[188] During his arrest in the northern coastal town of Luquillo—undertaken by twenty-four FBI agents supported by snipers and a helicopter—Ojeda Ríos shot at least forty rounds from an Uzi and a pistol at agents, wounding one before a sniper shot the gun out of his hand and he was taken into custody.[189] Four years later, in August 1989, Ojeda Ríos successfully defended himself against charges linked to the shooting, with a federal jury in San Juan acquitting him, apparently convinced by his claim that the law enforcement officials arrived at his home to "assassinate" him.[190]

Amid such upheaval, the PPD's Hernández Colón defeated Romero Barceló in the November 1984 elections and returned to office the following year. Hernández Colón pushed for the island to retain its commonwealth status in relation to the United States, arguing that the island's economic development program, which had raised its per capita income from $342 in 1950 to $5,574 in 1989 (still less than half that of Mississippi, the poorest state at the time), "could not continue" if the island was granted statehood. He said this was due to the fact that as a commonwealth, "no federal taxes are levied on the island" and there were tax incentives encouraging manufacturing under commonwealth arrangements. In the *New York Times*, he wrote that "statehood would destroy our economic achievements and the possibilities of commonwealth, a noble experiment in flexible political relationships for people with different cultures."[191]

The impact of the decline of the sugar industry and shuttering of the oil refineries on living standards was brought tragically home in the early morning hours of October 7, 1985, when the impoverished hillside barrio of Mameyes outside of Ponce, where many were out of work, collapsed in a landslide after days of driving rain. At least fifty people died and some two hundred homes were destroyed.[192] By 1990, an astonishing nearly 25 percent of Puerto Rico's workforce would be employed by the island's government.[193]

On September 23, 1990—the 122nd anniversary of el Grito de Lares— Filiberto Ojeda Ríos cut off the electronic monitoring ankle bracelet he was obligated to wear while awaiting trial for his involvement in the September 1983 Wells Fargo robbery, and became a fugitive.[194]

4

BODEGA-SOLD DREAMS

By the early 1990s, Puerto Rico found itself once again buffeted by winds affecting the giant power that ruled it and over which it had little control. A new governor, Harvard-educated doctor and PNP member Pedro Rosselló, had assumed office in January 1993, but was unable or unwilling to significantly ameliorate the situation.

By the middle of the decade, Puerto Rico's public debt had ballooned to $15 billion.[195] As it was seeking new revenue with which to reduce the federal deficit, President Bill Clinton's administration, with both Democratic and Republican support, decided that the time would be opportune to abolish Section 936 of the Internal Revenue Code, which gave companies from the mainland US an exemption from federal taxes on income earned on the island, whether in the form of operations or interest on local bank deposits. The prospect of losing tax-exempt status raised alarm with the pharmaceutical, electrical equipment, and food processing factories on the island, but appeared to register little in Washington. Even in March 1993, when an estimated one hundred thousand people marched on the island to support retaining the code, its days already appeared to be numbered.[196] In the *Christian Science Monitor*, Representative Dan Burton, a Republican from Indiana, and Peter Deutsch, a Democrat from Florida, opined that "the US can truly help the Puerto Rican people and their leaders create new jobs and an overall better quality of life while at the same time saving the Treasury more than $5 billion by phasing out Section 936."[197]

Many in Puerto Rico, including Governor Rosselló, saw things rather differently, with the president of the Puerto Rico Manufacturers' Association telling the *New York Times*:

> We Puerto Ricans will have to participate in the President's call to sacrifice, but we are asking that our sacrifice be proportional to our economic situation and that additional unemployment not be created on an island where 18 percent of the people already are without jobs and the per-capita income is only one-third that of the mainland.[198]

Rosselló also predicted that the move would cause a "gigantic decline" in the island's economy, warning, "if we're already cutting programs because of a budget deficit, and we would have half a billion less, it would mean chaos."[199] Rosselló's PNP, though, generally supported the measure, seeing it as a piece of its desired move toward statehood. Moody's Investors Service also sounded the alarm, warning that getting rid of the section "could have long-term negative effects on the island's economy . . . slowing—possibly even halting—job generation."[200]

In August 1996, as President Clinton signed a bill raising the minimum wage, an end to Section 936 was tucked within the legislation as well. The island would be sacrificed to pay for the minimum wage hike on the mainland. A few days later, the lingerie factory operated by Crescent Industries, which sold its wares to Maidenform, announced that it was closing its factory in the western town of Aguada and moving to the Dominican Republic, leaving 987 people jobless. It was a warning of what was to come.

With the Small Business Job Protection Act of 1996, the corporate tax breaks for all factories operating under Section 936 on the island would disappear within a decade and no new federal incentives for investment would be forthcoming. Even Clinton appeared to be aware of the potential impact of the legislation he had just signed, warning that it "ignores the real needs of our citizens in Puerto Rico" and urging Congress to "reform" it.[201]

As clouds darkened its economic horizon, the security situation on the island also deteriorated. In 1999, drug lord José Figueroa Agosto would casually stroll out of prison after likely having bribed his jailers, and would spend the next fifteen years running a binational drug smuggling empire in Puerto Rico and the Dominican Republic.[202] Beginning in 1998, drug trafficking based in La Perla solidified under the leadership of Jorge Gómez González, who would later become the leader of the community development organization Asociación Pro Rescate y Desarrollo de La Perla. In contrast to the sometimes chaotic atmosphere that existed in previous years, Gómez González set up a system dictating where and how drugs could be sold, banning dealers not born and raised in La Perla from traversing the neighborhood without explicit permission (an actual yellow line painted on the ground demarcated a final barrier).[203] The group's main activity was distributing cocaine and heroin that was then fanned out to the caserios elsewhere on the island.[204] In most of the caserios, the drug trade was controlled either by the Organizacion de Narcotraficantes Unidos (ONU gang, also known popularly as La ONU) or their rivals, the Rompe ONU (ONU Breakers).

On December 13, 1998, the island held a referendum on its political status, with voters given the options to maintain Puerto Rico's commonwealth status with the United States, have a "free association" that would continue a legal connection with the United States but grant further autonomy, follow a process to ascend to statehood, opt for independence, or "none of the above." With a turnout of 71.3 percent, "none of the above" came out in the lead with 50.5 percent of the vote. After an intense pro-statehood campaign, the vote came as a stinging defeat to Governor Rosselló.[205] The following year, the island would present the last (constitutionally required) balanced budget it would see for fifteen years, and would embark on an orgy of borrowing in order to finance its deficits.[206] By this point, an outsized section of the island's economic activity was dominated by the government via a "complicated system of special privileges [including] licensing restrictions, multiple permitting processes, and several tax incentives."[207] Conversely, the government's very size, with its sprawling bureaucracy and manifold departments, had created a lack of transparency and accountability. A mordant term—*la pala* (the shovel)—had even gained currency as a way to describe the connections within the government and its various sprawling departments to get anything done on the island.

Rosselló left office in January 2001, bequeathing the island a public debt of some $25.7 billion.[208] He was succeeded as governor by the PPD's Sila María Calderón, who had served as San Juan's mayor for the previous four years, and who defeated the PNP's Carlos Pesquera and the PIP's Rubén Berríos to claim the prize. During the last two years of Rosselló's term, federal prosecutors indicted a slew of public officials on the island, including the PNP mayors of Toa Alta, Villalba, and Corozal and the heads of various NGOs and contractors. Allegations swirling around a San Juan AIDS institute tasked with using federal funds for the treatment of AIDS patients charged that the moneys had been redirected to both the PNP and the PPD at various points. At least $2.5 million had been embezzled from the commonwealth's Housing Department alone.[209] Subsequent arrests ensnared Rosselló's former education secretary, Víctor Fajardo, the island's Chamber of Commerce president, and others, with US attorneys charging that at least $1 million of $4.3 million in diverted federal funds found its way into PNP coffers.[210] Juan Manuel García-Passalacqua—a learned professor, political analyst, and former advisor to both Luis Muñoz Marín and Roberto Sánchez Vilella who had transformed into the foul-mouthed, caustic bane of the island's politicians and hosted a popular radio show on Noti-Uno—bemoaned "a population that votes blindly" for two political parties.[211]

Making it clear that she had different priorities, Governor Calderón (herself a scion of the island's elite) in 2002 began targeting almost seven hundred communities that comprised about one-fourth of the island's population. She poured $1 billion into a program designed to improve housing, roads, water, and electric services, as well as providing additional health and educational programs. The program was financed via a $500 million grant by the island's Banco Gubernamental de Fomento para Puerto Rico (BGF) and a $500 million long-term bond issue.[212] The larger question—why, fifty years after Puerto Rico became a commonwealth, nearly 50 percent of its citizens still lived below the federal poverty line and needed such assistance—was one neither the PPD or the PNP appeared to have the stomach to delve too deeply into. Adding to what had been accrued during Rosselló's tenure, between December 2000 and December 2006, under Calderón's governorship, Puerto Rico's total public debt increased from $26.18 billion to $45.88 billion, an increase of 75.25 percent. Between June 2003 and June 2004 alone, its central government debt increased from $6.89 billion to $8.52 billion, an increase of 23.7 percent.[213]

One of the issues that would most define Calderón's time in office was that of the island of Vieques, which by that point the United States had been using as a firing range for sixty years. On April 19, 1999, David Sanes Rodriguez, a thirty-five-year-old civilian employee of the US Navy working as a security guard on Vieques, was killed when a pilot accidentally dropped two five-hundred-pound bombs near the observation post where he worked, an error that injured four others.[214] After Sanes Rodriguez's death, protesters flooded the bombing range, setting up makeshift encampments that would remain for more than a year and halting further bombing on the island, using nothing more than their bodies, as long as they remained.[215] In early May 2000, about two hundred protesters were handcuffed by federal agents and led off the Vieques range (though not arrested as many had been before), including San Juan Bishop Álvaro Corrada del Río and Democratic representatives Luis Gutiérrez and Nydia Velázquez. At a protest attended by several thousand people in Old San Juan after the removal, attendees shouted *Fuera marina!* (Navy out!).[216] Once the protesters were gone, the Navy resumed its bombing of the island.[217]

Calderón had strongly protested the Navy presence on Vieques both during the campaign and after she assumed office.[218] As her mandate progressed, the situation grew ever more heated. By April 2001, as fighter jets continued to drop their bombs into what had once been a scene of tropical idyll, protesters took to the sea in small boats and sailed to the target area, leading to their arrest. Hundreds of protesters also cut through the fence at the US Navy's Camp Garcia and entered the facility, with some hurling rocks and cow dung at Navy guards who fought back with pepper spray and rubber bullets.[219] Finally, in June of the same year, President George W. Bush announced that the US military would be leaving Vieques because residents "don't want us there" and "the Navy ought to find somewhere else to conduct its exercises."[220] In May 2003, with Calderón in attendance calling it "a moment of great happiness and profound emotion," and four days of celebration declared across the tiny islet, the US Navy left Vieques. In a statement, the Navy said it had transferred the land to the Department of the Interior, whose responsibility it would be to clean it up.[221] In 2005, the Environmental Protection Agency designated parts of Vieques as a Superfund toxic site, which by law required that the Navy clean up its former bombing range.[222]

As Puerto Rico's woes seemed to multiply, a half-forgotten voice from its past still sporadically reappeared. On July 25, 2000, the 102nd anniversary of the US landing in Puerto Rico, Los Macheteros released another one of their increasingly infrequent communiqués. Referring to the nineteenth-century independence activist Eugenio María de Hostos, the group denounced "102 years of abuse . . . of violation of fundamental human and civil rights," the "pseudo-democratic mechanisms" of the state, and the "deformation of a people" and "cultural genocide" it said was being committed on Puerto Ricans. The group also expressed its support for the campaign of civil disobedience being carried out on Vieques, adding that "our silence is part of a conscious collaboration with the sectors that have pinned hope on the chances of success of the application of the concept of civil disobedience. . . . We hope that this conception can achieve the desired successes. However, we will have to keep our guard very high and ready to take revolutionary action in the face of negative signals."[223]

In an interview with WPAB 550 AM's José Elías Torres broadcast in mid-2005, Filiberto Ojeda Ríos—who, as a fugitive, had been absent from the nonviolent civil disobedience that eventually drove the Navy from Vieques—referenced the war in Iraq, developments in Venezuela, Martiniquais anticolonial intellectual Frantz Fanon, and Mexico's Zapatista movement while saying that Puerto Ricans had been "reduced . . . to believing that we cannot stand on our own. . . . That is a sense of inferiority that has been inculcated through a hundred odd years of American colonialism." He went on to deliver words that in some ways might be seen as an epitaph, both political and personal:

> We have to know our worth just like any other people, and we have
> to make the decisions at this time to get out of this situation. . . . As
> long as Puerto Rico is a colony, the armed struggle is valid. While
> Puerto Rico is not free, while Puerto Rico lives the oppression
> it is experiencing, while Puerto Ricans are suffering from all the
> repression—political, ideological, cultural—that we have suffered from
> the colonialists, armed struggle is vital and it is important. . . .
> We are not crazy, nor are we adventurous. . . . Every act that is done has
> a political objective. Each situation, each activity that is generated of

an armed nature must have a very specific political purpose. . . . For me
it was worth it. It has been worth it because I feel that, first, that I have
been useful to my country. . . . I feel satisfied, happy and this is my life
and I will take it to its culmination as I am and rendering the greatest
real revolutionary service for our people. . . . That is the feeling that I
charge and that is the spirit that I carry and I believe that with that I
will go to the grave. Because that is my life.[224]

In another era, it was the kind of message that might have resonated
in small towns like Hormigueros, which clung to the western mountains
just south of Mayagüez, and where Don Luis, as the white-haired man was
known, cultivated mangoes and bananas, occasionally sitting on his front
porch overlooking a fecund landscape with his wife late in the evenings.
The atmosphere of tropical lethargy was disturbed late on the afternoon of
September 23, 2005—the 137th anniversary of el Grito de Lares—by an
eruption of gunfire from both outside and within the house. As FBI agents
rushed around the structure, one was severely wounded. The FBI and "Don
Luis" exchanged fire several more times. At one point, a woman left the
building, unharmed, and was detained and released.[225] His wife now out
of harm's way, Filiberto Ojeda Ríos, severely wounded, bled to death inside
the house, as federal agents did not allow anyone to enter the building until
the following afternoon.[226]

Though very few had sympathy for Ojeda Ríos's violent methods, many
shared the opinion of the executive director of the Puerto Rico Federal
Affairs Administration in Washington, Eduardo Bhatia, who said that by
killing Ojeda Ríos on the anniversary of el Grito de Lares, the United States
had "created a martyr of the man."[227] FBI director Robert S. Mueller would
order an independent review of Ojeda's killing,[228] and the following year,
Puerto Rico's Justice Department sued US federal authorities, including
Mueller and Attorney General Alberto Gonzales, for their alleged role
in obstructing the investigation into the killing, charging that "the FBI's

position to refuse to provide the names of the agents and the other officials in question constitutes an impermissible interference" with the country's bilateral governing pact with the United States.[229] The lawsuit was eventually quashed by a US District Court judge who ruled that Puerto Rico did not have the authority to obtain FBI material, and a federal appeals court ruled that such information could jeopardize both FBI investigative practices and the safety of the agents themselves. The US Supreme Court refused to hear the case.[230] Though US law enforcement was free to operate throughout the island, there was apparently little local authority they were bound to respect.

Some five thousand mourners came to file past Ojeda Ríos's body as it lay in state at the Colegio de Abogados in San Juan. As the funeral cortege traveled to Ojeda Ríos's birthplace of Naguabo on the eastern edge of the island, some children en route waved plastic machetes.[231]

Following the earth-shaking events of the Navy's departure from Vieques and the killing of Ojeda Ríos, one could have been forgiven for hoping that Puerto Rico might be at the beginning of a new chapter and that better days might be ahead. Old habits die hard, however, as the tenure of Calderón's successor, the PPD's Aníbal Acevedo Vilá, would demonstrate.

Acevedo Vilá had previously served as the island's nonvoting member of Congress from 2001 to 2005, and the new governor's administration almost immediately confronted a severe economic crisis. By late April 2006, with the island's $1 billion deficit likely to see it run out of cash, leading to the potential shuttering of over fifteen hundred schools and the inability to pay over two hundred thousand public sector workers, Acevedo Vilá implored lawmakers to pass a bailout plan he was advocating. As nervous consumers lined up at supermarkets and gas stations amid rumors of impending strikes, the governor and opposition lawmakers that dominated the legislature spent weeks battling over the size of a proposed sales tax to cover a potential $638 million loan.[232] By mid-May 2006, only after mass demonstrations following the shuttering of forty-three government agencies (which put nearly one hundred thousand people out of work) and the closing of all schools on the island, a special commission designed to referee between the governor and legislators got the two sides to agree to an emergency loan.[233] By August 2008, however, Acevedo Vilá's government was asking for a $500 million credit line from the state owned Banco Gubernamental de Fomento para Puerto Rico to pay 120,000 public sector workers.[234] That same year, the Instituto de Estadísticas de Puerto Rico was created to provide independent data on the country after years of politically influenced meddling with official figures.

In March 2008, Acevedo Vilá was named in a federal indictment that accused him of a range of campaign finance violations, including using campaign funds to fly his family around the world on vacations and buying nearly $60,000 worth of designer clothing. Acevedo Vilá dismissed the charges as "totally false."[235] Though he would be acquitted on all charges the following year after a month-long corruption trial,[236] the charges and trials, coming soon after the scandals of the Rosselló administration, helped create the impression of an apparent addiction to shady backroom deals by both the island's major political parties that was hard to deny. Attempting to win a reelection campaign in the middle of fighting a legal battle, Acevedo Vilá went down in defeat to the PNP's Luis Fortuño, who like Acevedo Vilá had preceded his ascent to Fortaleza with a stint as the island's nonvoting representative in the US Congress, and who won 52.77 percent of the vote in the contest.

As 2008 began, Fortuño took office promising to rein in the soaring homicide rate, create thousands of private sector jobs, and reduce the island's tax burden, but he had been warned by advisors that within three months, the government might again run out of funds to pay public sector workers.[237]

The year 2008 would be Puerto Rico's deadliest in more than a decade, with 807 homicides surpassing even the previous year's sanguinary total of 728.[238] At least 1,430 metric tons of cocaine reached the island, helping Puerto Rico achieve the dubious distinction of being the largest transshipment point for US-bound cocaine in the Caribbean.[239] In January 2009, José Figueroa Sancha, a deputy director of the FBI in Puerto Rico who had been closely involved with the raid that killed Filiberto Ojeda Ríos four years earlier, was confirmed by Puerto Rico's Senate as the new superintendent of the Policía de Puerto Rico, having been nominated by Fortuño two months earlier. The changing of the guard seemed to have little impact on the human meat grinder of the island's drug trade, however, and as Sila María Calderón's mandate had largely been defined by the struggle over Vieques, Fortuño's would be marked by a steady drumbeat of shocking crimes. In late September 2009, three teenage boys were found shot to death on a basketball court in Loíza.[240] A month later, a massacre at the La Tómbola bar in Toa Baja killed seven and wounded twenty.[241] Alexis Candelario Santana, who had led the Palo de Goma drug gang in the area and was eventually convicted of orchestrating the killings, had been released from prison in Puerto Rico—after serving only six years and despite having pled guilty to more than a dozen murder charges—and had orchestrated the raid on the bar as revenge against his cousin, who he believed had unlawfully taken over his territory.[242] The police also had their own depredations to contend with, with images such as the videotaped murder by police officers of forty-three-year-old Miguel Cáceres Cruz at a quinceañera celebration outside Humacao contributing to the department's well-earned reputation for lethality.[243] A report by the American Civil Liberties Union found a pattern of excessive and lethal force against civilians, especially in poor neighborhoods, Afro-Puerto Rican neighborhoods, and communities of Dominican descent, as well as often violent suppression of peaceful protests and failure to protect victims of domestic violence.[244]

In his inaugural address Fortuño had warned that it was "time to control government spending,"[245] and in May 2009, his government fired eight thousand public sector workers. By late September, it confirmed that it would be firing 16,970 more by early November, a move that it said would cut $386 million in spending and was part of the effort to close the island's $3.2 billion deficit. With Puerto Rico grinding through a three-year recession and a 15 percent unemployment rate, union leaders and others clashed with police outside La Fortaleza on September 29. The same day, Fortuño was pelted with an egg as he tried to deliver a speech in Fajardo.[246] During his tenure, Fortuño would sign laws cutting the island's capital gains tax rate to zero for investments made by new residents and cutting the tax rate for new businesses on the island to 4 percent. This came atop Puerto Rico's already-low capital gains tax for current residents (10 percent as opposed to 23.8 percent on the mainland) and the fact that island residents would pay no federal income tax.[247]

On June 14, 2011, President Barack Obama would touch down in San Juan. He was the first US president to visit Puerto Rico since John F. Kennedy some fifty years earlier, and while the president's interest was heartening to some, the island's lack of security, coupled with its economic crisis, continued to be the chief concern of most residents. In October 2010, the FBI arrested seventy-seven police officers on the island, charging that they were aiding drug traffickers.[248]

A late June 2011 raid by US federal agents and Puerto Rican police in La Perla saw law enforcement breaking down doors and arresting 114 people on drug and weapons charges, including community leader Jorge Gómez González, president of the Asociación Pro Rescate y Desarrollo de La Perla, and Unión de Trabajadores de Muelles president Santiago Hernández Rosa.[249] Gómez González was subsequently sentenced to thirty years in prison on charges of conspiracy to possess controlled substances with intent to distribute.[250] The La Perla raid also provided an opportunity for the English-language press to regurgitate some of its hoarier clichés about the neighborhood, with one writer breathlessly describing the district as a "notorious" slum "where few venture unless they live there or seek to engage in illegal activities."[251] In a very Boricua twist on the international drug trade, in a separate operation, a well-known Santería priest was arrested along with several members of his cadre. They were charged with helping smuggle US-bound drugs onto Puerto Rico from the Dutch Caribbean island of Sint Maarten and with rigging the island's lottery system, while soliciting the help of a spirit named Samuel that would give them supernatural advice about their criminal enterprise.[252]

More unnerving than the drug busts, however, was the fate of New Jersey native Maurice Spagnoletti, the executive vice president of mortgage and banking operations for the money-hemorrhaging Puerto Rican financial institution Doral Bank. On June 15, 2011, Spagnoletti was riddled with bullets as he drove his black Lexus sedan on one of San Juan's busiest highways.[253] Nine shots from a .40-caliber handgun entered Spagnoletti's car as he waited in one of the capital's endemic traffic jams. Four entered his head. Though the shooting was by no means random, Captain Ferdinand Acosta of the police department's major crimes unit would later conclude that "the shooter exhibited poor aim, so he may not have been a professional gunman."[254] Seven years later, federal authorities would finally charge six suspected drug traffickers with the killing, saying that Spagnoletti had been targeted for investigating suspect bank transactions.[255]

The following month, José Figueroa Sancha, the former FBI official appointed by Fortuño to head the Policía de Puerto Rico a little over two years earlier, announced that he was quitting, with Fortuño citing unidentified "health problems." Under Figueroa Sancha's tenure, homicides on the island had soared and the police had been involved in serious abuses against university students, journalists, and union activists.[256] By the end of the year, the island would witness an astonishing 1,136 murders, the highest number of homicides it had ever seen.[257] Figueroa Sancha would be replaced by former National Guard officer Emilio Díaz Colón, who would last less than a year before resigning at the end of March 2012. Díaz Colón's business-as-usual approach, absence from high-profile police operations, and shyness with the media had come in for strong criticism by the island's legislators and others.[258] He would be succeeded by Héctor Pesquera, a former FBI investigator and a coordinator for the United States Department of Homeland Security at the Broward County Sheriff's Office in Florida, who had most recently served as head of security for the Port of Miami.

The staccato refrain of violence continued, though, and many worried their beloved island was entering the phase of the final breakdown of law and order. In November 2012, the storied boxer Héctor "Macho" Camacho became the latest victim of the island's roiling insecurity when he was shot in the face as he sat in the passenger seat of his friend Adrián Mojica Moreno's SUV in Bayamón, where he had been born fifty years earlier. Mojica Moreno died at the scene and Camacho was transported to a hospital, where he was declared brain dead and passed away four days later after being taken off life support. Ten bags of cocaine were found in Mojica Moreno's car.[259] Camacho's son, Hector Camacho Jr., lamented, "death, jail, drugs, killings, that's what the streets are now."[260] Days later, a well-known publicist, José Enrique Gómez Saladín, went missing after last being seen in San Juan's Condado neighborhood. Four days later, his burned body was found on pasture land near a disused correctional camp in Cayey in the central mountains.[261] Four young Puerto Ricans, two men and two women, would eventually be convicted of the murder, having carjacked Gómez Saladín and withdrawn $400 from his bank account. Four hundred dollars for a life.[262] The murder sparked a social media campaign using the hashtag #TodosSomosJoséEnrique (We are all José Enrique) that expressed exhaustion with the violence wracking the island, and in which celebrities such as Ricky Martin and the salsa singer Víctor Manuelle participated.[263]

It was amid such an atmosphere that Puerto Ricans went to the polls in November 2012. As voters on the mainland returned Barack Obama to a second term as president, voters on the island—who had little say in who became president of the colossal country that ruled them—voted by a slim margin in a nonbinding referendum to jettison their commonwealth status to become the fifty-first state in the United States. Strangely, however, both pro-statehood Governor Fortuño and the pro-statehood mayor of San Juan, Jorge Santini (who by that point had been mayor for twelve years), lost to defenders of the commonwealth status, senator Alejandro García Padilla and Carmen Yulín Cruz, who had served in Puerto Rico's Cámara de Representantes since 2009, respectively.[264] Asked to respond to two questions—whether Puerto Rico should continue with its commonwealth status and, if not, whether they preferred statehood, independence, or status as a sovereign nation in free association with the United States—for the first time a majority, 54 percent, said they did not want to continue with the current arrangement. 61.2 percent voted thusly opting for statehood, 33.3 percent chose free association, and a mere 5.5 percent voted for independence.[265]

An attorney and law professor by training, García Padilla entered La Fortaleza in January 2013, by which time successive governments in Puerto Rico had racked up a borrowing total of $29 billion since 2004.[266]

During the course of García Padilla's first year in office, life in Puerto Rico became increasingly expensive for the island's already-struggling lower and middle classes. With the island's general obligation bonds edging toward junk status, García Padilla's government imposed new taxes on businesses and on commercial bank transactions.[267]

The sinking of the island's bonds brought about the arrival of capitalist adventurers specializing in distressed assets, who availed themselves of the steep discount Puerto Rico's debt provided. Hedge funds—referred to scornfully by many on the island as "vulture capitalists"—lent Puerto Rico more than $3 billion, envisioning a 20 percent return on the back of the island's constitutional clause requiring that bonds be paid back. These funds were dominated by some of the most politically powerful people in the country. Paulson & Co., the hedge fund of leading Republican donor John Paulson (who had given $1 million to Mitt Romney's Super PAC Restore Our Future during Romney's presidential campaign and would later serve as an early endorser of and economic adviser for the presidential campaign of Donald Trump), swooped in. It was followed by Appaloosa Management, which had been founded by David Tepper, who lavishly backed both Republican and Democratic candidates and would be a supporter of former Florida governor Jeb Bush's ill-fated presidential run. Entities such as BlueMountain Capital Management, Marathon Asset Management, and Monarch Alternative Capital (whose founder, Andrew Herenstein, would host two fundraisers for Marco Rubio's unsuccessful presidential run) followed suit.[268]

By October 2013, Puerto Rico was $87 billion in debt, which accounted for about $23,000 for every man, woman, and child in the island's population. As a territory, it had no legal ability to declare bankruptcy, and repeated downgrades of the worth of its bonds had effectively shut it out of the bond market. The government was reduced to short-term bank credit financing and other schemes to stay afloat from month to month, effectively creating a pyramid scheme where the state was borrowing money from some lenders to pay others.[269] Between 2004 and 2013, the island's population fell from 3.8 million to about 3.6 million, a decline of 212,000 residents, or 5.5 percent of its total population.[270]

As 2014 began, unemployment was stalled around 15 percent, and those who did get a job could expect an average salary of around $15,200 per year.[271] A March 2014 report by the United States Government Accountability Office on the likely effects of statehood on Puerto Rico poured cold water on the possible exit ramp from the crisis that many on the island had just voted for, concluding that the federal government would end up having to pay billions more on programs such as Medicare and Medicaid and that "changes in federal program spending and to federal tax law under statehood could lead to economic and fiscal changes of their own in Puerto Rico . . . [which] may have a cascading effect on federal spending and revenue levels," though it admitted "the precise nature of such changes is uncertain."[272]

That January, I went down to Puerto Rico. Renting a car at Luis Muñoz Marín International Airport, I drove east, the blue-green Caribbean Sea splashing to my left, the tormented island fecund and seething on my right. At Piñones, I stopped at one of the roadside shacks that line the beachfront road like stray seashells and ordered *alcapurria*, the ubiquitous fritter dish stuffed with various kinds of fish, and drank *coco frío* straight from the shell only feet away from the water. Though it was relatively early in the day, I was surprised that I was the only customer. Continuing on south to Maunabo, the island's mountainous interior descended into the churning sea. I checked into a small hotel, the Parador MaunaCaribe, that fronted the ocean, and as I walked to dip my feet in the surf I was joined by a pack of docile stray dogs that roamed the beach, chasing one another and playing in the surf before coming to rest and sleep in the shade of a palm tree. Driving into the town, with the sound of the coqui frogs that have become a symbol of Puerto Rico filtering in with the warm breeze through the open window of my car, I found people sitting under a magnificent old tree in the town square, chatting and relaxing as the heat of the day dissipated under a blanket of stars. A nearby evangelical church was going strong, and at a sports bar, Rincón Jueyero, patrons chatted over a din of salsa music.

"It hasn't been easy," the woman behind the bar told me of the island's economic travails. "But we're surviving somehow."

The next morning I rose with the sun, ascending fiery from the sea at my door, and continued driving along the south coast and into the winding narrow roads of the western mountains. I passed through small mountain towns, somnolent and curiously devoid of people, the laughter of children replaced by empty main streets and "For Rent" signs on abandoned storefronts. Just before I reached Maricao, I happened upon a hotel just off the roadside, all but abandoned but for a single security guard to protect it from vandalism. Its rustic charm hinted at former grandeur, but it was gradually being overtaken by the tropical brush, the voices of any guests long since silenced. San Germán, the island's second-oldest city, sat lovely but decaying under a half moon.

As I drove through San Juan upon my return to the capital, I was greeted by an immense mural of Filiberto Ojeda Ríos on the side of a building in the Residencial Manuel A. Pérez caserio in the neighborhood of San José. Above a Puerto Rican flag, hands upraised, Ojeda Ríos gazed soulfully out at the street below, images of masked federal agents swirling around him.

That night, I sat with my friend Jacques-Christian Wadestrandt, a professor at Inter American University and the son of a famous rebel who tried to topple Haiti's dictator, François Duvalier, in 1964 and paid for that attempt with his life. Wadestrandt had largely grown up in Puerto Rico, raised by his mother, Sylvia Bajeux, and her second husband, Jean-Claude Bajeux, both well-respected human rights and democratic activists, and he had seen the island's gradual descent into the tangled and perilous state in which it now dwelled. At one of the alfresco bars that surround the iconic La Placita market in Santurce, we watched as a group of young men churned out bomba rhythm on drums called *barriles* while people laughed and flirted and tried, if only for a night, to forget about the sea of troubles that faced them.

"To be honest with you," Wadestrandt said, putting down his beer and taking in the scene, "I think the commonwealth arrangement has given everything it has to give."

Soon after my visit, the ratings agency Standard & Poor's downgraded Puerto Rico's debt to junk status, from BB+ to BBB-, saying it was no longer qualified for an investment grade and doubting the island government's ability to raise cash. The catch-22 of the downgrade, however, was that much of the island's debt was incurred with a promise to begin cash payments—in the neighborhood of $940 million—if the debt sank below investment grade. In a joint statement after the news broke, Puerto Rican Treasury Secretary Melba Acosta Febo and Chairman of the Government Development Bank David H. Chafey Jr. said they were "disappointed" by the downgrade but "confident that we have the liquidity on hand to satisfy all liquidity needs until the end of the fiscal year, including any cash needs."[273] The immediate impact of the move appeared less dire than feared, and though the island's bonds traded lower, no mass panic selling occurred.[274]

In a late February 2014 conference call with investors, government representatives said that the island still had the capacity to issue another $3 billion in new debt, which would almost entirely be used to refinance the island's existing debt. A successor to the island's bond-issuing entity, the Corporación del Fondo de Interés Apremiante (COFINA), which had been created in 2006 but by this point had burned through its entire capacity, was suggested but went nowhere.[275] By early April 2014, the island's Government Development Bank announced that it had hired the New York law firm Cleary Gottlieb Steen & Hamilton, which had previously represented such financially struggling nations as Argentina, Greece, and Iceland.[276] As the island's economy teetered, hedge funds sensed the opportunity for big returns. The higher the risk—not just for investors, but in terms of the fate of the island, as well—the higher the reward for speculators.[277]

Even as Puerto Rico's financial horizon appeared to dim, Governor García Padilla tried to paint a rosier picture, telling attendees at the Palm Beach Strategic Forum in Florida that "Puerto Rico is not Detroit and not Greece."[278] As if to underline his point, both Germany's Lufthansa Technik and Arizona's Honeywell Aerospace announced investments in the island of $20 million and $24 million, respectively.[279] At the end of April, the island presented its first balanced budget since 1999, when Governor García Padilla issued a balance sheet that saw a draconian $1.4 billion in cuts and adjustments. Though some—such as consolidating an unwieldy twenty-five government agencies—appeared sound, other moves, such as cutting agency budgets by 8 percent and promising $775 million to pay the island's debt—an increase of over $500 million more than the previous year—seemed unresponsive to the island's dire economy.[280]

At the Puerto Rico Investment Summit held in San Juan that April, John Paulson, the billionaire manager of the Paulson & Co. hedge fund, told attendees that the island could become "the Singapore of the Caribbean."[281] At the same conference, Governor García Padilla called on Spanish firms to invest in the island, citing "greater access to the US market than any country of Latin America. . . . With financial regulations like the US but outside the American tax system."[282]

In June 2014, Governor García Padilla succeeded in pushing the Public Corporation Debt Enforcement and Recovery Act through Puerto Rico's Congress, signing it into law on June 28. The act sought to create a proceeding similar to bankruptcy to restructure the debt of corporations held by the commonwealth's government. PREPA bonds responded by sinking to forty cents on the dollar. Some of Puerto Rico's municipal bond holders, including Oppenheimer & Co. and Franklin Templeton, immediately sued to block implementation of the law. More than $3 billion of Puerto Rico's general obligation and governmental development bank bonds could nevertheless not be restructured through its passage. Many took the law as a sign that the island was willing to let its publicly held companies, like PREPA and the Puerto Rico Aqueducts and Sewers Authority (PRASA), go under.[283] As July 2014 ended, Puerto Rico's $73 million public debt still loomed over the island.[284]

What had once been viewed as uniquely dire economic straits had grown even worse. During July 2014, economic activity on the island fell to a twenty-year low, the nineteenth month in a row that it had declined, with cement sales and gasoline consumption particularly hard hit.[285] In a speech delivered in Baltimore, Maryland, in early August, Kent Hiteshew, director of the Treasury Department's newly established Office of State and Local Finance, opined that Puerto Rico had "additional difficult choices ahead" but praised the commonwealth's "ongoing efforts to achieve fiscal stability and economic growth."[286] The following month, PREPA hired the New York-based consulting firm AlixPartners to help it restructure its $671 million debt to various lenders, payments that it could not meet and which the owed parties, including Citigroup, gave it more time to pay.[287]

Puerto Rico's economic worries largely overshadowed a piece of notable good news. In 2014, the island had witnessed 681 homicides, its lowest rate in almost fifteen years and a 40 percent drop from the record high three years previously,[288] though the number of Puerto Ricans obtaining licenses to legally carry firearms increased by 56 percent during the same year.[289] According to the Bureau of Alcohol, Tobacco, Firearms and Explosives, many of the high-powered weapons used in Puerto Rico's underworld were purchased legally in states with lax gun laws, especially Florida, and then smuggled onto the island.[290]

"We are experiencing a social, institutional, economic, moral and political bankruptcy at all levels," fretted columnist Benjamín Torres Gotay in *El Nuevo Dia*, before caustically observing that "those who have spent their lives preaching dependence, now insult those who depend. . . . Those who insult you are insulting themselves."[291]

There were flickers in the popular imagination that reminded people of the island's greatness. The 2015 musical *Hamilton*, envisioned by the Nuyorican playwright and composer Lin-Manuel Miranda and based on the life of another son of the Caribbean, US founding father Alexander Hamilton, spoke in accessible terms of a struggle for independence and respect that many Puerto Ricans found very familiar. Two years later, the video for the song "Despacito," by the singer Luis Fonsi and the reggaeton artist Daddy Yankee, shot the La Perla neighborhood in ravishing colors amid the Caribbean's tumbling waves and evoked the ebullient spirit that still existed despite all the struggle. This sense of ennui, though, was vividly reflected in the island's literature, in works such as Luis Negrón's 2010 short story collection *Mundo Cruel* and Eduardo Lalo's 2012 novel *Simone*, in which one character observes, "We're a half-formed country. . . . A society that's never been able to think of itself as anything but a province."[292]

At the beginning of 2015, with the island's financial outlook seeming ever more dire, Judge Francisco A. Besosa of the United States District Court in San Juan struck down key provisions of the Public Corporation Debt Enforcement and Recovery Act, signed into law by García Padilla the previous June. Saying the act exceeded federal law, Besosa forbid its continued implementation, considerably narrowing the options available to the island as it sought debt relief and sending the island's bonds sinking lower still. The government said it would appeal,[293] but the United States Court of Appeals for the First Circuit would affirm Besosa's ruling a few months later.[294]

Around the time of the Besosa decision, Puerto Rico's nonvoting member of the House of Representatives, Pedro R. Pierluisi, proposed a bill to allow the island's municipalities and public corporations (such as PREPA) to declare bankruptcy, bringing the island more or less into line with the rights enjoyed by most states. At first, the proposal seemed to be generating bipartisan support—the staffs of both Republican senator Marco Rubio of Florida and Democratic senator Richard Blumenthal of Connecticut began working to craft a bill reflecting Pierluisi's proposal, and Pierluisi's move also had the support of conservative organizations such as Grover Norquist's Americans for Tax Reform. However, the hedge funds and others that Puerto Rico owed money to—including mutual funds such as Franklin Templeton and Oppenheimer Funds—launched a full-court press against any relief. BlueMountain Capital representatives disseminated a letter to Republican congressional staffers arguing that "Chapter 9 proceedings bail out Puerto Rico on the backs of the very bondholders Congress incentivized to invest in Puerto Rican municipal bonds."[295] The national coordinator of the Tea Party Patriots, Jenny Beth Martin, whose own organization had come under criticism for its use of 501(c)(4) status,[296] and who personally enjoyed total annual compensation of over $450,000 for her advocacy of various right-wing causes,[297] railed that the proposed bill was "nothing but a backdoor, taxpayer-funded bailout for Puerto Rico."[298] The so-called "60 Plus Association," claiming to be "Main Street bondholder" senior citizens but in fact founded by the conservative billionaires Charles and David Koch, ran ads attacking García Padilla for "manufacturing a crisis" and trying to "extort" money from the federal government.[299]

As was his wont when confronted with a hint of displeasure from either his right-wing political base or his wealthy funders, Rubio eventually caved and abandoned his support for the measure, writing instead that "the same liberal ideology that has wreaked havoc on the broader U.S. has had far more disastrous consequences for Puerto Rico" and, in a brazen turnaround from policies he himself had been advocating only weeks earlier, opined that "allowing Puerto Rican municipalities to reorganize their debts under Chapter 9 of the U.S. Bankruptcy Code would not solve Puerto Rico's problems and should only be a measure of last resort considered if Puerto Rico takes significant steps to fix its budget and economic mess."[300] He was joined by Utah Republican senator Orrin Hatch, whose recent political ambitions had also been lavishly funded by firms with investments in Puerto Rico, and who blocked an effort to even bring the Pierluisi bankruptcy legislation to a vote, instead offering another $3 billion in exchange for which Puerto Rico would submit to federal oversight of its finances, another stripping away of the island's already-modest autonomy.[301] The Nobel Prize–winning economist Joseph E. Stiglitz summed up the attitude of the island's creditors thusly: "They want their money now, and they want to get the rules set so that they can make money for the next 20 years."[302]

In April, by a twenty-eight to twenty-two vote, Puerto Rico's Congress rejected García Padilla's plan to overhaul the island's tax system in an action that the governor responded to by issuing a statement charging the House of Representatives with "putting into danger the continuity of public services, the retirement system, debt payments and health services."[303] Every month, Puerto Rico's government had to cleave off $93 million from its meager resources as it was constitutionally required to pay its general obligation bonds before any other expense.[304] In early May, a report from Puerto Rico's Government Development Bank raised the specter of a possible moratorium on debt payments, given the possibility of the government running out of money during the first quarter of fiscal year 2016 barring any new revenue, including for public programs and services.[305] The island's citizens, meanwhile, continued to feel the squeeze, and in May, thousands of Universidad de Puerto Rico students and their supporters marched to La Fortaleza to protest proposed budget cuts.[306] As the summer went on, the government increased the island's sales tax from 7 percent to 11.5 percent.[307]

In later June, only days before the first of Puerto Rico's multimillion-dollar debt payments came due, García Padilla told the *New York Times* that the island's debt was "not payable" and that it was in a "death spiral." Adding that things would be "bad" for creditors who would not renegotiate payment terms, he said that they had to heretofore "share the sacrifices" of the island's long-suffering population.[308] A report finding that García Padilla's government was commissioned to look into the island's financial situation (and which became known as the "Krueger Report," after one of its authors, former World Bank chief economist Anne O. Krueger) appeared at the end of June, warning that "government deficits . . . over the coming years imply an unsustainable trajectory of large financing gaps" and concluding that the island's true fiscal deficit was "much larger than assumed" before advocating bridging this with "a voluntary exchange of existing bonds for new ones with a longer/lower debt service profile."[309] After the report's release, the

New York Times weighed in on its editorial page, urging support for the Pierluisi bill.[310]

Amid warnings that the island could head down the path of utter collapse that Greece had experienced, a host of economists argued that Puerto Rico urgently needed an option to avail itself of bankruptcy protection.[311] By late July 2015, however, billionaire hedge fund managers connected to entities such as Aurelius Capital, Davidson Kempner Capital Management, and Fir Tree Partners that held $5.2 billion of Puerto Rico's debt seized upon a report they themselves had commissioned by a trio of former International Monetary Fund economists to demand the island lay off yet more teachers and close more schools in order to pay back its debt.[312] Titled "For Puerto Rico, There is a Better Way" and prepared by the Centennial Group, the report breezily suggested a number of measures to cut expenses by $2 billion over five years, including "reduce number of teachers," "reduce subsidy to University of Puerto Rico," and "cut excess Medicaid benefits."[313] The report omitted the fact that, though school attendance had fallen from 765,000 to 573,000 during the previous decade, the island's education spending per student—$8,400 per year—was still well below the US national average of $10,667.[314]

The island managed—just barely—to make a $169 million payment for the debt service on its bonds on July 31,[315] but as August began, it missed a $58 million bond payment.[316] That same month, it was revealed that *Mi Salud*, as Puerto Rico's version of Medicaid was called, owed providers around $200 million and had lost access to credit.[317]

Dozens more schools would close around the island during 2015.[318] By the end of the year, the total number of schools closed over the previous five years would rise to more than 150.[319] During the summer of 2015, more than 1.5 million people on the island were impacted by the worst drought to hit the Caribbean in years.[320] In the mountain town of Lares, where the first major revolt against Spanish rule had begun nearly 150 years earlier, more than a quarter of businesses had closed as nearly two thousand had left in the preceding four years. More than four thousand had left the decade before that. Entire neighborhoods took on a ghostly and abandoned air.[321] In another seeming ill omen, at the end of December 2016, Guarionex Candelario Rivera, a police officer who had been on sick leave, arrived at the Ponce police precinct where he worked and shot three colleagues to death before being shot by police. He would subsequently be sentenced to two hundred years in prison.[322]

As Christmas approached, García Padilla told reporters that it was "very, very unlikely" that the island would not default on debt due January 1, telling reporters at a San Juan event the government was debating "if a partial payment is to be done, which bonds should be paid?"[323]

As 2016 began, the island did indeed default on around $174 million in debt payments to lower-ranked creditors in order to, in theory, pay general obligation bondholders first, as stipulated in the island's constitution. When asked about the apparent shell game with the island's debts, García Padilla said, "It's very simple. We don't have money to pay." Standard & Poor's responded to the move, known by the financial industry term of art as a *clawback*, by downgrading the rating of Puerto Rico's infrastructure authority's rating from CC to D and cautioning about the "great uncertainty as to Puerto Rico's true financial position."[324]

In response to the clawback, Assured Guaranty Corporation and the Ambac Assurance Corporation, both of which had insured Puerto Rico's bonds, sued the island, claiming the government had illicitly diverted at least $163 million earmarked to pay its debts. García Padilla responded by continuing to sound the alarm, calling on Congress to provide Puerto Rico with bankruptcy protection and saying that "swift action from our congressional leaders is necessary and what the people of Puerto Rico deserve" and that the lawsuits showed that "litigation pandemonium" loomed.[325] He had earlier warned that "every dollar that I need to use to pay lawsuit lawyers will be a dollar that I will not have available to pay creditors."[326]

Though President Barack Obama had floated the idea of giving Puerto Rico greater autonomy to write its debts down in federal court (similar to the power enjoyed by local municipalities), by late February 2016, with the deadline looming in little more than a month, Republicans in the US Congress had begun to openly suggest federal oversight of the island's finances, further eroding what little autonomy the island did enjoy, and balked at the idea of giving the island control over restructuring its debt.[327]

On April 6, in a move designed at least in part to protect the Government Development Bank's rapidly depleting coffers, García Padilla signed a bill into law that allowed him to impose a moratorium on debt payments on the grounds of "fiscal emergency." At the signing, he strongly criticized investors and the US Congress for blocking the government's previous attempts to resolve the island's debt. At the time of signing, the Development Bank had only $562 million in liquidity and was staring down a $400 million payment due in May. Days before the bill signing, a group of hedge funds had sued the bank to stop it from forgiving debt.[328] The funds, including Brigade Capital Management and Claren Road Asset Management, claimed that the Government Development Bank had withheld financial information and intended to initiate "preferential transfers" to creditors before paying the funds themselves off. The GDP's President Melba Acosta Febo called the charges "erroneous," even as the lawsuit offered further proof, she said, that Puerto Rico's financial situation was "dismal" and its debts "unpayable," before calling again for a federal debt-restructuring regime.[329]

On April 11, García Padilla unveiled yet another new plan, which agreed to pay holders of general obligation bonds at a rate of seventy-four cents on the dollar, with those creditors deemed less important getting even less. The move was envisioned to cut $49 billion of the island's debt down to somewhere between $32.6 billion and $37.4 billion. One creditor dismissed the offer as a "sideshow."[330] Days later US District Judge Gustavo

Gelpi ordered Puerto Rico's government to pay bills—some of them years old—owed by its Health Department to the island's mentally ill, saying that, without the payments, "the effects to these individuals will be devastating and beyond repair."[331]

After an early May visit to the island, Arizona Representative Raúl Grijalva, the ranking Democrat on the House Natural Resources Committee, was so disturbed by what he found that he called on Congress to either pass legislation or send humanitarian aid, stating that, though "people talk about a bailout. . . . There is no money being talked about extended by the United States government."[332] That same month, participants in the Universidad de Puerto Rico's medical school's deferred compensation plan voted to liquidate the fund's $103 million of assets before they could (theoretically) be seized by creditors if the school became insolvent.[333] By late May, the Republican-controlled US Congress began pushing a plan that would create a seven-member board that would oversee the island's debt restructuring and have veto power over the island's budget and a plan for "fiscal responsibility." The idea of Puerto Rico's government prostrate before an unelected group tasked with defending the legal rights of creditors could hardly evoke a more colonial instrument of pressure.[334]

In early June 2016, a seventeen-member commission appointed by Puerto Rico's legislators released a forty-four page report that suggested that some of the island's debt might have been issued in violation of its constitution (by issuing loans for terms of more than thirty years, for example). The report went on to suggest that the government might not, in that case, be responsible for repaying it.[335] As June dragged on with no deal and default loomed, García Padilla wrote in an editorial that the island would "default on more than $1 billion in general obligation bonds, the island's senior credits protected by a constitutional lien on revenues."[336]

A sixty-eight to thirty-two vote in the US Senate on June 29 passed the Puerto Rico Oversight, Management, and Economic Stability Act (PROMESA) with a filibuster-proof majority from senators of both parties. Despite the criticism of both senators of the left (Bernie Sanders and Elizabeth Warren) and the right (Ted Cruz), in a spirit of pure colonialism, it established an overnight board—the Financial Oversight and Management Board (FOMB)—for Puerto Rico with the power to restructure the $70 billion debt that had stalked the island for years. Democratic Senator Robert Menendez of New Jersey called the bill "the ultimate neocolonialism," and said, "It treats the citizens of Puerto Rico like subjects."[337] Describing the legislation before the Senate as "a horrific bill," Sanders went on to say that it "[took] away all of the important democratic rights of the American citizens of Puerto Rico. . . . Basically, four Republicans who likely believe in strong austerity programs will essentially be running that island for the indefinite future."[338] A number of senators had called for amendments but were told by Senate Majority Leader Mitch McConnell and Treasury Secretary Jack Lew that there was no more time, with McConnell painting a dystopian picture of the island having to "lay off police officers, shut down public transit, or close a hospital" if the Senate didn't act.[339] At the beginning of July, the island defaulted on $800 million in payments to holders of its general obligation bonds. The money wasn't there to both pay the bondholders and keep the island functioning, García Padilla said, so he had made the choice "to ensure the residents of Puerto Rico continue to receive essential services while the commonwealth continues to face a delicate financial situation."[340]

The following month, President Obama announced the seven members of the oversight board, three Democrats and four Republicans selected from lists submitted by the House leadership, four of whom were of Puerto Rican descent. They would not be paid. Among the board's member were former Chief Judge of the United States Bankruptcy Court for the Southern District of New York Arthur J. Gonzalez, former Santander Puerto Rico CEO and Oriental Financial Group Senior Executive Vice President José Ramón González (he also served as president of the Puerto

Rico Government Development Bank), and José R. Carrión, an executive at insurance brokerage firm Hub International, who would become the board's chairman. All but one were men, the lone female being former California Department of Finance director Ana J. Matosantos.[341] The FOMB quickly called for litigation brought by creditors to pause while it sorted through the island's debt.[342] Despite the island's financial woes, in late October, the Puerto Rico Public Housing Administration (PRPHA) pledged $65 million to make the island's public housing more accessible to disabled residents.[343]

As the FOMB met at a luxury hotel in Fajardo on November 18 at a six-hour rendezvous that was closed to the public, dozens of protesters wielding Puerto Rican flags swathed in black marched into the body's offices in San Juan, denouncing what they charged was the board's "dictatorship."[344] In a clear sign of rebellion, on November 21, 2016, Governor García Padilla announced that he would not comply with the new board's first demand, that he submit a new fiscal plan that took into account what the board viewed as the absence of federal financial help. García Padilla refused, saying, "it's not right, and it's not necessary. . . . That would push us into an economic death spiral. It would mark a return to policies of depression."[345]

Either way, García Padilla would not be in office to see those policies in action, as he declined to run for reelection. As 2017 began, Ricardo Rosselló, the son of former governor Pedro Rosselló, assumed the governorship of the troubled island. A PNP member like his father, Rosselló studied at the Massachusetts Institute of Technology and the University of Michigan, earning a PhD in biomedical engineering from the latter. In 2010, he cofounded a China-based medical company, Beijing Prosperous Biopharm, which investigated drugs to treat a variety of illnesses, including prostate cancer, brain tumors, and HIV.[346] Returning to Puerto Rico in 2011 after a stint as a researcher at Duke University, he began writing a column for the *El Vocero* newspaper and, the following year, founded *Boricua ¡Ahora Es!* (Boricua, Now It Is!), a political advocacy group somewhat quixotically dedicated to uniting the island's three ideological strains (commonwealth, statehood, and independence). The group had actively campaigned for a "no" vote on maintaining the island's current commonwealth status during the 2012 referendum.[347]

Pedigreed scion of the island's ruling class or not, the island's demons had little intention of giving Rosselló any sort of a honeymoon. In late March 2017, Ukraine's former Minister of Finance Natalie Jaresko became the FOMB's executive director at a salary of $625,000 a year. As Jaresko was born and raised largely in Illinois and spoke fluent English, the appointment was not as far afield as it might have at first appeared; however, her salary did raise some eyebrows. FOMB chairman José Carrión defended it, citing Jaresko's "world-class experience" and suggesting that Ukraine was in similar dire straits when she took the financial helm there in 2014 (though Ukraine was helped out with $40 billion from the IMF to speed its recovery).[348] When the FOMB met in New York—not San Juan—in April, members mulled over a series of proposals that advocated, among other measures, closing the Government Development Bank, increasing the price island residents would be charged for water, and privatizing the electricity supplier. Only hours later, Rosselló went on television to announce that he would sign a bill promising an array of taxes on new items and limits on vacation and sick days.[349]

Privatizing the island's public services had the potential to create one hundred thousand new jobs and pump $5 billion into the island's moribund economy, Rosselló told hundreds of investors attending a two-day April conference in the capital, saying that he realized the government "can't do everything." Eyed for privatization were everything from the operation and maintenance of highways and ferry services to waste management and natural gas. The government said that it had no other choice as it did not have access to capital markets, and that it simply could not take the lead in terms of cash outlay on investment projects.[350]

On May Day 2017, thousands of protesters flooded roads around the island, blocking traffic to protest the grinding, seemingly endless austerity crisis and the proposed austerity measures. Some chanted, "Ricky is selling the island!" Police eventually launched tear gas and pepper spray against a small group that shattered bank windows in the capital.[351] As the order that protected the territory from lawsuits expired at the beginning of May, a group representing bondholders who had purchased $16 billion worth of bonds filed a lawsuit charging that the government's plan to cut or reduce its debut was unconstitutional.[352] In a sign that *la pala* was still in effect, a few weeks later Rosselló fired four of the seven board members of the Instituto de Estadísticas de Puerto Rico, the body created a decade earlier and tasked with providing independent data to the government that was free of political influence, replacing them mostly with people who had been employed by the government either directly or as contractors, a move many saw as violating the body's autonomy. All appointees had financially contributed to Rosselló's campaign for governor or to the PNP.[353] Two were later annulled by Puerto Rico's courts.[354]

By May 2017, the island's Secretary of Education, Julia Keleher, announced that it would be necessary to close an additional 179 public schools and reassign twenty-seven thousand students, saying the government had "spent ten years handing out nearly $3 billion in a system that hardly has any books" and that it could not "keep doing what we're doing because we don't have the resources." The closures came in addition to the 150 schools that had been shut down between 2010 and 2014. Many parents only found out about the closures through media reports, and many students would be changing schools for the second time in as many years.[355]

After the Universidad de Puerto Rico's administration unveiled a plan to increase tuition based on a family's ability to pay at the school, where a full course load cost less than $1,700 and students paid no tuition at all thanks to federal Pell grants (many even got a subsidy for living expenses), students erupted in protest, effectively closing several campuses down.[356] The president of the university's board of trustees, Dr. Carlos Pérez Díaz, resigned on May 23—the second in his position to do so in a year—rather than face potential jail time for failing to reopen the school, which by that point students had kept closed for two months in protest against education cuts recommended by the FOMB, which sought to slash its budget in nearly half. Pérez Diaz's exit followed those of a number of other members of the board of trustees.[357]

Meanwhile, the island's creaking power grid showed signs of ever greater strain, with the previous years having seen more than fifty-four thousand people report power failures, an increase of 24 percent from just two years earlier. PREPA had lost 22 percent of its workforce since 2014. A report the utility commissioned characterized its capacity as "barely able to provide electric service with its present fleet," noting that it "dispatches its units with software that was developed in 1985," and described its approaches to problem-solving as "often improvised, with results that are disastrous as often as they are admirable."[358]

The power grid would have fewer and fewer people to serve. Between 2009 and 2017, the number of homeless people on the island increased 10 percent, according to the US Department of Housing and Urban Development.[359] By mid-June 2017, an average of fourteen families a day were losing their homes on the island to foreclosure, a rate that had doubled in only a decade. A record 5,424 homes had been foreclosed on the previous year, though the actual number was thought to be much higher as local banks frequently sold defaulting loans to companies in the mainland United States, where the cases were largely handled by federal courts.[360]

A June 2017 referendum on the island's status—the third since 1998—was sullenly boycotted by the PPD, and only 23 percent of eligible voters, most of them supportive of the PNP, participated, which perhaps explained the fact that 97 percent of those who voted opted for statehood.[361]

While the economic vise tightened, the old squabbles about identity endured. But thousands of miles away, over the Atlantic Ocean, something was churning that would tear off the veil of the colonial relationship once and for all.

5

MARIA

ON SEPTEMBER 12, 2017, A WELL-DEFINED TROPICAL WAVE—AN elongated area of low air pressure rumbling westward accompanied by a coterie of clouds and thunderstorms—appeared off the west coast of Africa, where the ancestors of many of Puerto Rico's citizens were seized from, and began rolling across the Atlantic. By September 16, it had become a named Tropical Storm—Maria—and by September 18, as it churned onto the island of Dominica, it had become a major Category 5 hurricane with sustained winds of 160 miles per hour.[362] That night, Dominica's prime minister, Roosevelt Skerrit, posted a series of increasingly alarming social media updates that began with "The winds are merciless! We shall survive by the grace of God!" before announcing, "My roof is gone. I am at the complete mercy of the hurricane. House is flooding." (His final post of the night said simply, "I have been rescued."[363]) Skerrit may have survived, but the devastation wrought by Hurricane Maria on Dominica was a precursor of what was to come. On September 20, the storm roared onto Puerto Rico.

Though the island had endured powerful hurricanes before—most notably 1928's San Felipe Segundo hurricane and the San Ciprian hurricane of 1932—nothing had prepared island residents, who had been struggling so mightily just to survive for so many years, for what was to befall them.

In the southeastern town of Yabucoa, near where the storm made landfall with winds reaching 165 miles per hour, 99 percent of the municipal buildings collapsed. The town's mayor, Rafy Surillo, characterized the scene as one of "total destruction" and said the community was "totally isolated" from the rest of the island.[364] In Guayama, a little more than twenty miles to the southwest along the coast, the Río Guamaní overflowed its banks, sending people from the barrio called Borinquen fleeing their homes. As communication to the town collapsed, so did its main supermarket.[365]

The neighborhood of Punta Figuera in Ceiba, on the northeastern coast, simply ceased to exist, so utterly destroyed was it by the storm.[366] Of the forty-nine structures there, most belonging to impoverished fishermen, all were nearly totally destroyed, leaving only chickens idly pecking the soggy ground in the storm's wake.[367]

In Toa Baja, west of San Juan, at least eight people drowned, including a family of a father, mother, and two children. As in nearby Levittown, whole neighborhoods were submerged. At least four thousand people had to be rescued.[368] In the Juana Matos neighborhood of Cataño, across the bay from San Juan, 80 percent of the homes were destroyed.[369]

In Utuado, three elderly sisters died when earth loosened by the intense rains collapsed onto the house where they were sheltering.[370] In the San Lorenzo barrio in the mountain town of Morovis, residents were left isolated when the storm's winds blew a temporary bridge away that connected them with the rest of the town, leaving the heartiest among them no choice but to wade across a sometimes swiftly moving river or walk an hour around it into the town.[371] After fifteen inches of rain soaked the surrounding mountains, a large crack appeared in the Guajataca Dam in the island's northwest, and engineers expressed fears that it would "collapse any minute."[372] The island's Servicio Nacional de Meteorología issued a flash flood warning for the towns of Isabela and Quebradillas, but, miraculously, the damn held.[373]

In the hours that the storm roared across the island, 80 percent of Puerto Rico's crop value was erased, some $780 million in agriculture yields.[374] Eventually, the Puerto Rican government would conclude that the hurricane had done $43 billion in damage to the island, with losses for the private sector alone totaling $30 billion.[375]

As officials on the island hunkered down, grimly suspecting what might await them once they emerged, Abner Gomez, Puerto Rico's emergency management director, told reporters, "Once we're able to go outside, we're going to find our island destroyed."[376]

And so it was. When residents of Fajardo finally emerged, they found streets full of felled trees, overturned cars, and shattered glass. Most of the homes in the Vista Hermosa and Barriada Roosevelt were destroyed. Mayor Aníbal Meléndez said he had "never seen the city so shattered."[377] Puerto Rico's resident commissioner Jenniffer Gonzalez told reporters, "the devastation in Puerto Rico has set us back nearly twenty to thirty years. . . . The Puerto Rico of now is different from that of a week ago. The destruction of properties, of flattened structures, of families without homes, of debris everywhere. The island's greenery is gone."[378] Rosselló told reporters that the storm had been a "major disaster" that had left "extensive damage" across the island.[379] With 1,360 of the island's 1,600 cell phone towers down, along with 85 percent of above-ground and underground phone and internet cables, two days after the storm, the island's government had still not been able to secure communication with forty of the seventy-eight municipalities on the island.[380]

Around the island, it became routine to see dozens or even hundreds of people gathered around buildings with generators or even parked along the roadside in search of WiFi or telephone signals, desperate to get in touch with relatives on the mainland.[381] In Guayama, the son of mayor Eduardo Cintrón arrived from Caguas to help with relief efforts and recorded video of the devastation with his phone to share once he found a signal. Once he did, the images were shared on the social media pages of the telenovela actress Karla Monroig, who hailed from the town, bringing attention to its plight.[382]

At the Las Teresas retirement community just outside San Juan, the administration left before the storm hit, leaving residents on their own, in the dark and without water, for over a week until they were discovered by a group of volunteers working for the municipal government.[383] At San Juan's Hospital del Maestro, patients groaned in pain due to a shortage of medicine and supplies; doctors said that by the afternoons the building would get so hot that "it's almost impossible to handle."[384] A Wisconsin doctor who returned from assisting relatives on the island warned a local newspaper that he believed "hundreds" were dead. His words would prove to be prophetic.[385]

As Puerto Rico (and the neighboring US Virgin Islands) faced down the most devastating natural disaster in their modern history, President Donald Trump spent a leisurely weekend at his private golf club in Bedminster, New Jersey, only rousing himself from his torpor to make a quick trip to Alabama to appear at a rally in support of the Senate ambitions of accused sexual predator Roy Moore. Though he met with acting Homeland Security secretary Elaine Duke at the golf club to discuss his proposed travel ban against citizens of several majority-Muslim nations and briefly touched on Puerto Rico, the two would not speak about the storm again until the following Tuesday, after precious hours and days had been lost.[386] Trump spent most of the weekend ranting on Twitter against North Korean leader Kim Jong-un[387] and "son of a bitch" players in the National Football League staging protests during the playing of the National Anthem.[388] Two days after the storm, a reporter landed at Luis Muñoz Marín International

Airport to find "no military air traffic control units on the tarmac directing plane loads of aid supplies, no bustling command center sending convoys of trucks to hard-hit areas, no mountains of relief goods stacked and ready to be deployed where needed." The only mainland response he could find was one FEMA employee smoking a cigarette outside the arrivals terminal.[389]

On Monday, five days after the hurricane made landfall, White House Homeland Security Adviser Tom Bossert and FEMA Administrator Brock Long were the first senior administration officials to arrive on the island. That same night, Trump dined with a group of conservative activists at the White House but, after briefly mentioning Puerto Rico, descended into a tirade about Republican senator John McCain. The first Situation Room meeting on federal and local efforts to respond to the storm would not happen until the following day.[390]

"We've invaded small countries faster than we've been helping American citizens in Puerto Rico and the Virgin Islands," Representative Darren Soto, a Florida Democrat and the first lawmaker of Puerto Rican descent elected to Congress from that state, acidly noted.[391]

On September 25, the Trump administration said that despite the devastation across the island, it would not waive the federal restrictions on foreign ships transporting cargo there, with the Department of Homeland Security (DHS) arguing that there was sufficient capacity for US flagged vessels alone to move supplies. DHS had previously waived the Jones Act in the wake of Hurricanes Harvey and Irma after they battered the East Coast of the United States. House Democratic Minority Leader Nancy Pelosi called on Trump to deploy the US military to aid with relief efforts, while Republican Majority Leader Paul Ryan issued a statement saying island residents would "have what they need."[392] On September 26, Trump waived a requirement that Puerto Rico contribute money to the federal emergency fund.[393]

As the president and his advisers dithered, desperation on the island grew. The following day, most supermarkets and restaurants remained closed amid the lack of power, and those that did open had long lines as people tried to purchase what sustenance they could from the nearly bare shelves.[394] In the surfing mecca Rincón, which had run out of the last of its potable water four days after the hurricane, mayor Carlos López Bonilla issued a desperate plea to authorities via satellite phone that people were "being driven to despair" and that the municipality looked "as if a nuclear bomb" had been dropped on it.[395] Ingel "Bori" González, the mayor of the northern coastal town of Río Grande, said the community had received no assistance from the island's government and, though the municipality was doing what it could to help people, residents were becoming "desperate" as food was "really scarce." He also pleaded for help for those residents who required oxygen tanks and ventilators to survive.[396] As he sought aid at the airport in Aguadilla, San Germán mayor Isidro Negrón warned that "we have people without oxygen in their homes and we have no way of filling these tanks. . . . We already have people who have died because they did not have oxygen. As for dialysis, we are transporting people to dialysis centers."[397]

In the northern town of Montebello, about an hour's drive west of San Juan, there was no sign of FEMA or anyone else from the federal or island government a week after the storm hit. A local cattle rancher helped provide water that allowed people to stave off dehydration. People bathed and washed clothes in a local river.[398] On Vieques, patients requiring dialysis watched as its only medical center was devastated, and would eventually be flown on thrice-weekly flights to the main island, an exhausting trip for the already enfeebled. A mobile dialysis unit purchased by federal officials for the island remained stuck in California for months (Puerto Rico's legislature had not paid the $3 million to have it delivered). A number of patients on the island died.[399]

With most ATMs nonfunctional as a result of the absence of electricity, islanders also began rapidly running out of cash, and found long lines at the few machines that did work.[400] One of the few sources of information for locals was WAPA 680, a San Juan radio station, whose old analog equipment required less power from a generator than the digital equipment most radio stations use. Before communications collapsed, the station fielded desperate calls from islanders trapped on their rooftops by rising floodwaters or otherwise trying to avoid succumbing to the storm. Afterward, medical professionals took to its airwaves to offer advice and counseling.[401]

Finally, on September 28—more than a week after the storm made landfall—the Trump administration announced that it would waive the Jones Act, with White House press secretary Sarah Huckabee Sanders communicating the news via Twitter, the administration's favored mode of communication.[402] Despite claiming multiple times that it was in fact Rosselló who was in charge of the overall response, a week in the Trump administration appeared to view the devastated island as a suitable laboratory for experimentation, with Homeland Security Adviser Tom Bossert saying a "business model" was being implemented that embedded federal officials in local municipalities, to coordinate with mayors and the heads of various utilities, unlike during previous disasters when federal authorities would allow local officials to direct resource distribution. FEMA, it was said, would lead the federal support effort, while the Defense Department would support civilian authorities.[403] Trump, for his part, after boasting of the "incredible job" his administration was doing, promptly left the White House for another extended weekend at his golf club in Bedminster.[404]

Six days after the storm hit, on September 26, the job of resurrecting the island's devastated electrical grid was doled out—via a $300 million no-bid contract signed with PREPA—to Whitefish Energy, a Montana-based company with exactly two full-time employees. The company would soon claim it had 280 workers, the vast majority of them subcontractors, working on the island, and that the number was growing by up to twenty new hires a day. PREPA had declined to activate the "mutual aid" agreement with other utilities that had been used after hurricanes Harvey and Irma, even though, in the case of Florida Power & Light (FPL), for example, teams had assembled to assess damage in Puerto Rico and provide assistance, an offer they were not taken up on. Whitefish took its name from the Montana town that served as its base of operations, a town that also happened to be the hometown of US Interior Secretary Ryan Zinke, who denied playing any role in helping the company secure the contract.

Whitefish was paid an initial $3.7 million upfront to cover "mobilization of personnel and equipment." The previous year, its entire annual revenue had been listed in procurement documents as $1 million.[405] PREPA chief executive Ricardo Ramos admitted that he had never heard of the company before but "we checked them out on the internet. . . . They showed a lot of experience in using helicopters to build transmission lines. On paper, they did have the experience necessary." Ramos also said the company did not demand a large advance payment to begin work, unlike many other firms.[406]

Several weeks later, when San Juan Mayor Carmen Yulín Cruz weighed in on the Whitefish contract, saying that it should be "voided right away and a proper process which is clear, transparent, legal, moral, and ethical should take place," the company responded saying, "we share [the] frustration. . . . But her comments are misplaced." Yulín Cruz responded by tweeting that if "asking for transparency is 'misplaced,' what [is Whitefish] afraid we will find?" On an island where the vast majority of people were still plunged into darkness once the sun set, the company then threatened the mayor, tweeting, "We've got 44 linemen rebuilding power lines to your city & 40 more men just arrived. Do you want us to send them back or keep working?"[407]

More than a week after the storm, Army Lt. Gen. Jeffrey Buchanan was selected to coordinate the government's military response to Maria and said frankly that there were "not enough" troops and equipment on the ground in Puerto Rico. When grilled about the delay in appointing Buchanan,

Bossert bristled that "it didn't require a three-star general eight days ago," something that must have come as a surprise to Puerto Ricans.[408]

By September 28, Trump's acting head of Homeland Security, Elaine Duke, said the situation in Puerto Rico was "really a good news story in terms of our ability to reach people and the limited number of deaths that have taken place in such a devastating hurricane." When CNN played Duke's comments, Carmen Yulín Cruz responded live on air by telling viewers:

> Maybe from where she's standing it's a good news story [but] when you're drinking from a creek, it's not a good news story. When you don't have food for a baby, it's not a good news story. . . . I would ask her to come down here and visit the towns and then make a statement like that, which, frankly, is an irresponsible statement. . . . This is, dammit, this is not a good news story. This is a people are dying story. This is a life or death story. This is there's a truckload of stuff that cannot be taken to people story. This is a story of a devastation that continues to worsen.[409]

After Yulín Cruz's statement, Trump, a man whose being seemed animated by the basest racism even in normal times, used Twitter to attack the island and its political leaders as it struggled to get back on its feet, tweeting on September 30:

> The Mayor of San Juan, who was very complimentary only a few days ago, has now been told by the Democrats that you must be nasty to Trump. . . . Such poor leadership ability by the Mayor of San Juan, and others in Puerto Rico, who are not able to get their workers to help. They want everything to be done for them when it should be a community effort. . . . 10,000 Federal workers now on Island doing a fantastic job. The military and first responders, despite no electric, roads, phones etc., have done an amazing job. Puerto Rico was totally destroyed.[410]

After Trump's Twitter outburst, Yulín Cruz went back on CNN the following night, this time wearing a black T-shirt that read, "Help Us We Are Dying," and told journalist Anderson Cooper, "We're dying here. We truly are dying here. And I keep saying it, S.O.S. If anyone can hear us, if Mr. Trump can hear us, let's just get it over with and get the ball rolling."[411] Responding to a shouted question about Puerto Rico from a reporter while speaking on the South Lawn of the White House following the massacre of fifty-eight people by a gunmen in Las Vegas, Trump said he would give the federal response to Hurricane Maria "an A+."[412]

Nearly two weeks after the storm hit, Trump finally visited Puerto Rico. His performance left many wondering whether it might have been best had he never set foot there at all.

At 11:43 a.m., he and the first lady Melania Trump landed at the Muñiz Air National Guard Base within the grounds of Luis Muñoz Marín International Airport. At almost the same time, the USNS Comfort, a ship often called a "floating hospital," arrived on the island. Later, seated around a long table with various Puerto Rican officials around him—Ricardo Rosselló was at Trump's right, wearing a frozen grin—Trump said that the governor "didn't play politics. . . . He told it like it was, gave us the highest marks" before going on to joke, "I hate to tell you, Puerto Rico, but you've thrown our budget a little out of whack because we've spent a lot of money on Puerto Rico, and that's fine."

At the press briefing that followed, Trump's tone became even more caustic, saying that the hurricane not been "a real catastrophe like Katrina" and then engaging in a Q & A where he gave false responses. When asked, "What is your death count?" he responded, "Sixteen people certified. Sixteen people versus in the thousands. You can be very proud. Sixteen versus literally thousands of people. Everybody around this table and everybody watching can really be proud of what's taken place."[413] Trump then made the short trip to a church in the relatively affluent San Juan suburb Guaynabo, where he was taken on a brief walking tour by the city's PNP mayor, Angel Pérez Otero, who fawned over the visiting head of state, telling him, "Your people are doing the right stuff for us. . . . Thank you, thank you, Mr. President."

The pair and their entourage then went to the Evangelical Calvary Chapel, where they were greeted by several dozen people, some of them carrying "Let's Make Puerto Rico Great Again" signs. Trump—who had earlier in the day falsely claimed that Puerto Rico's power grid had been "devastated" even before the storm hit—handed out flashlights to some members of the crowd, muttering, "You don't need them anymore, you don't need them anymore."[414] And then, in what would become the iconic moment of his visit, he picked up some paper towels and began tossing them into the crowd. It was a frivolous gesture that befit the boorish, buffoonish, deeply insensitive, and incurious man who made it. During the entirety of his visit, he would not leave the San Juan metropolitan area. When Air Force One took off at 4:08 p.m., he had been on the ground for less than five hours.[415]

A few miles away from where Trump had been boasting, in the neighborhood of Playita, Associated Press reporter Danica Coto found a neighborhood "stacking fallen tree branches, pieces of zinc roofing, and sewage-soaked clothes in shopping carts, and dumping them on street corners alongside piles of wet mattresses." Residents said they had not seen any federal assistance since the storm hit.[416] Almost concurrently with Trump's visit, the Environmental Protection Agency was still warning that "raw sewage continues to be released into waterways and is expected to continue until repairs can be made and power is restored. . . . People should not use the water from rivers, streams, and coastal water to drink, bathe, wash, or cook with unless first boiling this water for a minimum of one minute. If boiling the water is not possible, water may be disinfected with bleach."[417]

In Caguas, ten miles to the south of the church where Trump appeared, twelve hundred homes had been partially or completely destroyed, and communication was still so impacted that the mayor and his staff had to regularly drive into San Juan to personally plead for aid.[418] In the badly damaged La Perla barrio just beneath Old San Juan, residents of both communities had begun providing a community dinner in a loaned space every night—neighbor helping neighbor—because, as one resident said, "You couldn't find food anywhere."[419]

By early October, in Canóvanas, east of San Juan, patients were arriving at clinics with signs of what medical staff thought might be leptospirosis—an infection directly linked to exposure to rat urine, which some believed had contaminated a spring that residents were drawing water from. At least one man died.[420] Eventually, the mortality database of the island's demographic registry would list at least twenty-six people as having died from leptospirosis in the months after the storm, twice as many as the previous year. A number of those who died had worked on relief efforts and had been in regular contact with flood waters.[421] In Aguadilla, a team of doctors arrived from Orlando's Florida Hospital and found conditions so devastated that they were unable to conduct CT scans, and could only complete X-rays by stepping outside and holding the film up to the sunlight. They watched a forty-two-year-old man—whose fever rose to 107 degrees—die before their eyes as they were unable to cool him.[422]

Even two weeks after the storm, in seaside Añasco, just north of Mayagüez, residents were forced to live amid a fetid goulash of dead cows, goats, chickens, and horses bobbing in still-standing flood waters and try to avail themselves of a nonfunctioning sewage system.[423] In Coamo, in the south-central mountains, only 15 percent of the population had access to potable water, and the municipal government was attempting to deliver water and canned food house-to-house by hand. At least 130 people were being housed in local schools. The town's mayor, Juan Carlos García Padilla, said he could no longer wait for federal aid and hired five private companies to help the municipality clear its roads. He spoke of patients with various medical conditions who had died in the community in the wake of the storm.[424] In the countryside around Utuado, some families were subsisting on homegrown yuca and plantains.[425] By mid-October, at least five thousand people were still living in temporary shelters in the island's schools alone.[426] Early on the morning of October 12, Trump roused himself to tweet, "We cannot keep FEMA, the Military & the First Responders, who have been amazing (under the most difficult circumstances) in P.R. forever!"[427]

Nothing on the ground supported Trump's assertion. On October 23, Lt. Gen. Jeffrey Buchanan and FEMA's regional administrator Thomas Von Essen landed a helicopter in Ceiba and told residents that fifty thousand more blue tarps would be arriving over the next week and that these would be distributed to mayors, along with five hundred generators that were positioned on the island before the storm. But this was a lie. FEMA did not have five hundred generators on the island before the storm. It had twenty-five. The agency had also only prepositioned twelve thousand tarps on the island before the storm. After Maria hit, FEMA cycled through two companies that did not bring a single tarp to the island, before settling on a third, Master Group, that specialized in importing hookah tobacco. Though some tarps did eventually arrive, they failed a subsequent quality-control inspection. The story about the generators was one of a series of falsehoods that FEMA would use to try and explain its own failure, including claiming that it took two weeks for surpluses to arrive in Morovis because the roads were closed (they were not). Internal documents later revealed that a quarter of the staff FEMA brought to the island would later be classified as "untrained" while another quarter would be judged "unqualified."[428] (By late June, FEMA would distribute 126,000 tarps.[429])

A subsequent FEMA report reviewing its response to Maria concluded that the agency had radically underestimated the amount of food and water that would be needed in the wake of the storm and was slow to grasp the logistical difficulties that would arise from getting supplies to the island after the fact. The satellite phones that FEMA sent to the island didn't work in the Caribbean. Former FEMA director Craig Fugate visited the body's San Juan warehouse shortly after the storm expecting to find food and instead found "empty shelves."[430] Months later, at least ten trailers containing relief supplies—including water, food, and baby supplies—were discovered infested by rats in the parking lot of a state election office in San Juan. Donated by nonprofit groups and private entities, the supplies had been distributed by the National Guard but their designated distributors apparently lost track of them as the crisis wore on.[431]

A little over three weeks after the storm had hit, I landed in Puerto Rico to survey the damage and write a series of articles on the recovery efforts. As we began our descent, we could see the azure waters of the Caribbean rolling in to kiss the shore, and that, miraculously, the foliage of the island had sprung back up from the ground to wreath it in green once again. Hundreds of containers sat stacked up at the various port facilities along the southern portion of the Bay of San Juan. Exiting into a vibrant blast of humidity, I was collected curbside by the photographer Nydia Meléndez Rivas, herself a native of Maunabo, with whom I would spent the next several days touring the island.

We drove southeast in the bright afternoon light, passing abandoned, devastated supermarkets, and drove through nonfunctional stoplights as we headed toward the spot where the storm had made landfall. Driving through Yabucoa, we stopped to grab a quick bite at a restaurant where many neighborhood residents had gathered to recharge their cell phones, since it had a generator, before wandering outside to try to find that elusive signal that would enable them to communicate with relatives back on the mainland.

As we began the descent down toward Maunabo and the sea, signs of the recent devastation abounded. Telephone poles lay on their sides, some having crashed down through the middle of houses, and electric poles looked bent near double by the wind. Their cables lay strewn chaotically along roadsides and in trees. In one field, an old school bus that the storm had picked up and flung some five hundred feet rested upside-down like a child's toy. Old stone homes, some of which had stood for over a century, had been reduced to mere piles of rocks. Driving the winding path to Maunabo's dock, we found it almost totally destroyed, with two fishermen and a stray dog glumly surveying what remained.

The dock had been modernized and refurbished just before the storm. Nearby, a small fishing boat named *Esperanza*—Hope—bobbed on the waves.

"I am a fisherman and the president of the Fisherman's Village, at least what is left of it," Victor Lam told me.

"Truly, I had never seen a hurricane as strong as this one among the ones that had hit Puerto Rico," Lam continued. "The waves came up to there." He pointed to a height easily above the head of a person.

"When we could finally come out there were fish everywhere."

We drove to a local gymnasium where a group of volunteers were working with the Puerto Rican National Guard to distribute food, and one *guardia* asked me if I was from FEMA. He looked disappointed when I told him no.

In the relatively impoverished neighborhood of Calzada, the scene was still one of devastation, with hunks of concrete from which wires jutted out menacingly—too big to be moved without equipment—laying along the roadside. With no electricity in their homes, many residents had gathered at a small bar being run off one generator. A group of men seeking refuge slapped dominoes down on one of the tables.

The bar's owner, Marcia Montes, a thirty-three year-old who had moved back to the island from California seventeen years earlier, told me: "It felt like an earthquake. Every time there was a gust of wind, you could feel your house shaking. There's not one house in this barrio where the windows didn't explode. I know a lot of people who lost everything. There's no communication. . . . People have to figure out where they'll find water.

They go to rivers."

As late-afternoon clouds descended low and appeared to threaten more rain, one place where people were heading was just down the hill from Montes's bar. There, hundreds of people waited in line at a public school to receive food thanks to the Chefs for Puerto Rico initiative of the Spanish-American chef José Andrés.

"If we had asked permission from above, we would still all be still waiting," Andrés had told me during a phone call just before I left for the island. "The private sector there is functioning very well, the bakeries are producing, the main food distribution companies have food, but the problem is they have to feed the island and no one is making the calls. Even in the worst of situations, all people want is a humble plate of hot food."[432]

And so it appeared. By this time, Chefs for Puerto Rico had already delivered about 2.2 million meals to the residents of Puerto Rico, more than any other body including FEMA and the Red Cross.

"There are many situations going on through Puerto Rico's municipalities, but Maunabo has been hurt deeply," said Edwin Pagan Bonilla, who was working at the kitchen and whose pro-statehood organization, Generacion 51, had partnered with José Andrés's network. "This is an effort that has risen from the community, but we need all the help we can get."

As the rain grew steadier, I walked back up one of the hills of Calzada to again take in the panorama of the town. Hundreds of houses, many with roofs gone, most with windows broken, were held in sodden ground beneath a dark sky. All of a sudden, behind me, I heard a stirring and turned to see what it was. In a devastated home across the potholed street where I stood, a beautiful white horse wandered defiantly, grazing, as if oblivious to the destruction around him.

We drove through mists of rain and stayed that night at the Hotel Lucia Beach, a simple oceanfront parador in Yabucoa. Most of the other guests appeared to be relief workers from private agencies. Very few appeared to speak Spanish. With the clouds holding low, the night was embraced by a starless black sky, and it was not until the next morning, rising with the dawn, that I saw the decimated beachfront we were facing. Dozens of trees had been felled and those remaining looked bent and weary, as if exhausted from the struggle they had undergone.

We drove on to Guayama, once the heart of the island's sugar industry and the site of Pedro Albizu Campos's epochal 1934 speech. En route we forded damaged bridges skirting swollen rivers where wild horses frolicked in the water. In the Palmas Bajas neighborhood of Guayama, we found the elderly Lucy Alvarado and her husband, Luis "Pucho" Gonzales, who told me they thought an apocalypse might be upon them when the storm landed.

"I experienced Hugo, Hortense, and Georges," Alvarado, a seventy-five-year-old rail-thin woman with a blue handkerchief tied over her head, told me, rattling off the names of previous powerful hurricanes that battered the island. She stood in the backyard of their half-destroyed home, clouds of mosquitoes buzzing infernally. "But there was never anything to compare to Maria. . . . People are crying, people are without hope."

As the outbuilding of her main home was destroyed by wind and rain, other parts of the house were battered. The storm tore a nearby basketball court from pillar to post, sending debris flying through the air like missiles. When the winds abated, they found the district had been sealed off by fallen trees and swollen rivers. Pucho had gathered their neighbors together to clear a path using machetes, shovels, and their bare hands.

"We had to get out," Gonzales, a vigorous-looking seventy-year-old man, told me as he stood in what had been the rear of their house, its roof and windows now gone. "We had to get moving so we banded together to free the neighborhood."

When night fell, save for candles, they were plunged into sweltering blackness. With mice and rats hunting through the darkness, the couple had found an unexpected ally to keep them at bay. Days after the storm hit, a stray kitten wandered into the battered home. Alvarado decided to let her stay. She named her Maria.

A few neighborhoods away, in Barrio Olimpo, we found seventy-year-old Veronica Tirado sitting in a house filled with memorabilia of that most American pastime, baseball, and photos of her son-in-law, the Major League Baseball pitcher Ricardo Bones. As with Lucy Alvarado and Pucho Gonzales, her neighborhood had not had electricity since the night of the storm, and only had water very sporadically.

"I thought the winds were going to explode the door," she told us of the night of the storm, the ubiquitous hum of mosquitos never far from our ears. "It has been a horrible experience, both during and after. I don't understand why we're still without light, why we're still without water."

Planning on heading further inland to the mountains, we stopped at another café; this one in a half-shuttered strip mall. As with the restaurant in Yabucoa, the presence of a generator meant the place had become a community hub of sorts, as people came both to get a hot meal and to try to recharge their phones and other devices. Over the café's soundsystem, a song by the Puerto Rican reggae band Cultura Profética was playing, its lyrics seeming to speak to the island's sense of abandonment by the current occupant of the White House:

Le da igual, desde su oficina.
Le da igual, tu calidad de vida
Le da igual, desde lo alto todo
Le da igual y nada cambia porque
le da igual, tiene la llave pero
le da igual, si no le afecta claro
Le da igual, desde su lodo todo
le da igual, la verdad

(He does not care, from his office

He does not care, your quality of life
He does not care, from the top everything
He does not care and nothing changes because
He does not care, he has the key but
He does not care, if it does not affect him clearly
He does not care, from his mud everything
He does not care, really)[433]

I had seen the US response to the January 2010 earthquake in Haiti firsthand. Within hours of the catastrophe, two thousand Marines had been dispatched from Camp Lejeune, North Carolina. Within days, the US Navy aircraft carrier USS Carl Vinson appeared in the harbor of Haiti's capital, Port-au-Prince. Shortly after, more than one hundred members of the 82nd Airborne landed and began handing out food, water, and medical supplies, and rapidly the number of troops grew to three thousand. It was clear that no such urgency was forthcoming on behalf of the citizens of Puerto Rico—even though they were US citizens, and even as austerity had left their own government in a far weaker position to respond to the storm. The difference in approaches was striking and dismaying.[434]

As we headed into the mountains toward Aibonito (which sat nearly twenty-five hundred feet above sea level), the tropical torpor of the coast lifted somewhat. We could see flowers blossoming again along the roadside, and at one turn a young couple sat on a swing overlooking an achingly beautiful valley. In one of the cultural quirks that one frequently finds in Puerto Rico, Aibonito had hosted a Mennonite community from the mainland United States for decades, and two of its number, a married couple named Harry Nussbaum and Linda Ulrich Nussbaum, ran a guesthouse there. The Casa Ulrich, as it was called, was run out of a building constructed in 1915, where Linda, a native of Illinois, had lived off and on since the age of nine as her father worked on various agricultural projects in the area. The Mennonites had also worked with the local community to help residents develop economically, aiding people with their dreams of opening everything from food carts to car washes. The Nussbaums' home, a simple but beautiful structure painted white with green trim, sat on a small hill that now boasted an uninterrupted view of virtually every structure for miles around.

"We didn't know we had so many neighbors before Maria took all the leaves off the trees," Harry said, drolly.

"You couldn't recognize the area after the storm," said Linda, as we sat on their veranda, the sun's fading rays pleasingly illuminating cottony clouds as it sank into the sea.

"The response was very slow," Linda continued. After Hurricane Hugo [in 1989], the blue tarps arrived immediately. This time there were no tarps. Getting gas was a major issue."

That week, the Nussbaums were planning to host a group from the Mennonite Disaster Service, which was bringing a team of construction workers to help repair the town's damaged homes.

As the sun set Nydia and I drove to the center of town to get a read on the place. The central plaza, battered though it was, still looked lovely at twilight and, against all odds, on an island where some 80 percent remained without electricity, the center of Aibonito had succeeded in restoring power to its urban core. As a result, people from all around the area had come and were sitting around, chatting, eating, or drinking. Many of the men were coming off hours working with municipally organized crews clearing debris. There was a feeling of collective catharsis following the day's work—even in the midst of a terrible trauma. Several stray cats and dogs, always conspicuously well cared for in Puerto Rico, also gathered to survey the action. Later that night, at a restaurant in a lovely old converted colonial building, I watched as a band played and the crowd sang along passionately with the lyrics of "Preciosa," a song made famous by the singer Marc Anthony. It recounts the island's many charms, from its beaches to its fragrant flowers, before ending with the emotional refrain, *Yo te quiero,*

Puerto Rico (I love you, Puerto Rico).

As we drove out of town the next morning, among the shuttered and damaged buildings we passed, one was a shuttered *escuela de danza*, whose sign indicated it had once offered jazz, salsa, and hip-hop instruction. Across its balcony, someone had strung a banner.

Y si el cielo cae, bailo bajo la tormenta, it read. And if the sky falls, dance under the storm.

In a mid-October interview, Rosselló said that $490 million in labor and another $740 million for materials and equipment would be needed to restore the island's power grid, but that he was confident at least 30 percent of customers would have electricity by the end of the month.[435] However, a month after the storm, 80 percent of the island still lacked power and 30 percent was still without water. Schools had not yet reopened, and only a little over half of bank branches were functioning. Though most super-markets had reopened, many carried only the most haphazard selection of nonperishable supplies. Almost five thousand people continued to live in shelters, where rainwater was the *eau de toilette* of choice.[436] For months after the storm, the island's aqueduct and sewer authority was forced to use trucks to transport used water from its pumping stations to treatment plants, as sixty-four pumping stations remained inoperable due to the absence of electricity and failures in emergency generators.[437]

Doctors at the Centro Médico de Río Piedras warned that the constant interruptions in electricity to the complex—including in the operating room—were putting patients' lives at risk.[438] By the end of October, after FEMA had issued a statement threatening not to cover the Whitefish deal and with most of the island still sitting in darkness as PREPA generated only 30 percent of its normal output, the Rosselló government cancelled Whitefish's $300 million contract to rebuild the island's power grid.[439] Finally, more than a month after the storm, utility crews from New York and Florida were slated to be sent to the island. The decision by PREPA to decline to activate the "mutual aid" agreement with other utilities that generally was invoked as a matter of course after natural disasters would remain one of Maria's enduring mysteries.[440]

In early November, PREPA executive director Ricardo Ramos declined to testify before the House Committee on Natural Resources, saying he was too busy trying to restore the island's power grid to attend. San Juan Mayor Carmen Yulín Cruz also declined to appear.[441] Ramos did, however, appear at the Senate Energy and Natural Resources Committee meeting a week later, where he said that "after reviewing about a half-dozen proposals from potential first responders . . . only two offered the immediate services that PREPA needed. One proposal required a guaranteed payment of $25 million, the other—from Whitefish—offered PREPA the ability to pay only for work that was completed (and mobilization/demobilization)."[442] By the end of the month, Ramos would resign, with Yulín Cruz tweeting, "That Ricardo Ramos does not head PREPA is the right thing. That he helped destroy the credibility of the PR government is a disgrace."[443]

Puerto Rico's colonial status continued to chip away at efforts to provide its citizens with any relief. Unlike in Texas and Florida, the federal cap on its food stamps program put in place in 1982 meant that increasing access to the program was not an option on the island, like it was in US states. It was forbidden from evoking the disaster relief section of the federal Supplemental Nutrition Assistance Program, despite the entire island being designated a federal disaster area.[444]

Like a vampire eternally rising from its crypt and dripping with menace, PROMESA again reared its head in the aftermath of the storm, with the FOMB and Republican lawmakers insisting that the junta have oversight control over any relief money. "Why?" Governor Rosselló asked as he appeared before Congress, as it was "not their role." Judge Laura Taylor Swain of the Southern District of New York largely agreed with Rosselló. She ruled that the FOMB had no authority to impose austerity or appoint new leadership at PREPA, as the latter's bondholders demand that it do.[445]

In testimony before the House Committee on Natural Resources, the FOMB's executive director Natalie Jaresko issued a stark warning:

> The hard truth is that the Island now needs help—emergency and restoration funds and assistance on an unprecedented scale. Before the hurricanes, the Board was determined that Puerto Rico and its instrumentalities could achieve balanced budgets, work its way through its debt problems, and develop a sustainable economy without federal aid. That is simply no longer possible. Without unprecedented levels of help from the United States government, the recovery we were planning for will fail.[446]

As 2017 neared its end, nearly half of Puerto Rico's residents—more than 1.5 million people—remained without power.[447]

Just before Christmas, *El Nuevo Día* columnist Benjamín Torres Gotay visited Morovis and found a place "stopped in time":

> Bridges demolished, cars crossing rivers. Neighborhoods incommunicado. Families living crowded together because homes that were lost have not been repaired, nor have their tenants received help to relocate. Total darkness. Very little water.

The residents there, many of whom lived below the poverty line before the hurricane, were washing their clothes by hand and cooking with firewood. They told him, stoically, that they were "waiting for whatever God wants."[448]

6

BRINGING OUT THE DEAD

At night, Old San Juan, for so long the nexus of the island's joie de vivre and filled with locals and tourists partying, mingling, and flirting until the wee hours, was mournfully silent and still. Its stores were shuttered and all but a handful of restaurants and bars were closed. The street cats that had lived for generations off the generosity of local residents trotted its darkened lanes and sat watchfully on its colonial steps, their forms cast by moonglow in arabesque shadows on the walls and pavements.

Shortly after the storm, I found myself sitting in Old San Juan one night with my friend Keiko Niccolini. She was on the island working with the US nonprofit Feeding America and the New York City-based food rescue organization City Harvest to facilitate a food donation organized by Mostafiz ShahMohammed, an old college friend of ours who ran a Manhattan private investment firm. I was staying at the Casablanca, one of the few hotels functioning in Old San Juan, and we sat and talked over pizza and wine at the Pirilo restaurant, which seemed to be virtually the only place open in the neighborhood. With the private sector and local actors once again delegated to fill in for a largely absent federal government, Niccolini told me that she had found the Banco de Alimentos de Puerto Rico, Feeding America's local partner, "very efficient." She had driven to Aguadilla, on the island's western edge, and back that day, seeing devastation along the entire route. The restaurant was filled with relief workers—most of them, as I had found in Yabucoa, from nongovernmental organizations—blowing off steam. Afterward we walked the streets, passing windows and doors that were shattered and through which the wind sighed mournfully, the warm air still caressing in spite of the melancholy.

Many shuttered stores bore handwritten notes expressing a variation of the phrase, *A todos nuestros clientes, por el momento estamos cerrados. Se levanta!* (To all our clients, for the moment we are closed. Rise up!) At the Centro de Estudios Avanzados de Puerto Rico y el Caribe, another hand-written note listed the curtailed hours of operation. On one door, someone had scrawled, *Mas amor por favor* (more love please). We drank rum at a tiny bar that was able to function thanks to a small generator it had set up, which was roaring in the middle of the street. We wondered to each other what the human cost of what we were seeing would be.

The question of how many people died in Puerto Rico as a result of Hurricane Maria and the federal government's arctic-hearted inaction in its wake was one that would be debated, often bitterly, for some time. Anyone who saw the island in the storm's wake knew that the initial reported total of sixteen dead was preposterous. But how many did die? And who was to blame?

I met Cynthia García Coll, a psychologist and visiting professor at the Universidad de Puerto Rico, at a Starbucks in Hato Rey months after the storm. I had to thread my way there carefully as all the streetlights outside were still not functioning, leading San Juan's drivers, adventurous risk-takers in normal times, to make the streets of the capital where one could pick up a decent clip of speed a muted demolition derby of near-misses and frazzled nerves.

García Coll had ridden the storm out in her condo in Dorado, about thirty minutes west of San Juan, and when she was finally able to go outside, she was stunned by the devastation.

"Everything that we took for granted was gone. No water, no electricity, no fresh food," she told me, as we sat, lounge jazz playing over the sound system, looking out at a rush of sun-blasted traffic outside.

> What keeps us together as human beings are routines, and those routines were gone, compounded by the uncertainty of not being able to communicate with your family here or in the United States. Basic needs took huge amounts of time. You would stand in line for gasoline for six hours. You would stand at a bank for two and half hours to get a little bit of money—because they wouldn't give you much—so you could buy ice and food, which was also very limited. Long lines under the sun, then blackout at night. The mosquitos were awful, people couldn't sleep because it was so hot and full of mosquitos.

Like others, she was appalled even more by the aftermath than by the hurricane. "The lack of response was worse than the hurricane," she told me.

> The first helicopter I saw here was six weeks after the storm. If there had been immediate response, it would have been a completely different story. What Maria did, no one was protected. People who had diabetes and renal patients and those who had cancer just died and died and died.

Among those who died were some of the citizens of the town of Isabela, which clung to the northwest corner of the island and before the storm had been so replete with flowers that it was called *el Jardín del Noroeste* (the Garden of the Northwest). Jaclyn De Jesús, a native of Isabela, had been studying for her PhD in clinical psychology at Carlos Albizu University and had ridden out the storm in San Juan. She returned to her hometown two days after Maria struck. The drive, normally a ninety-minute trip, took her eight hours as she traversed the debris-strewn roads. Once there, she found some of the town's elderly and infirm residents completely cut off and waiting for death.

"Most of the old people had family living outside Puerto Rico, living in the States," De Jesús told me months later, as she was packing up and preparing to move to California, like so many Puerto Ricans, forced by economic reality to leave her beloved island.

> They had had nobody. You would go into a house and find them. In one house, a woman was bedridden and her husband was trying to care for her. They were waiting for days with no way of contacting anyone, for someone to help them. The entire community came together and tried to lend a hand, but we found at least two people who had died, and we had to bury them in their backyards because there was nowhere else to take them. And as far as I know, they're still there.[449]

Another one of those claimed by the storm, although from a completely different milieu, was the San Juan artist Heriberto González. One of the pioneers of digital art on the island since the 1980s, Gonzáles, with his distinctive long hair and beard, had for years been a fixture in the galleries, bars, and streets of Old San Juan. He played music in the Puerto Rican folk genre, designed album covers, and even authored a book of science fiction tales, *Selene: relatos fantahistóricos y otros cuentos lunares* (*Selene: Fantastic Tales and Other Lunar Stories*), in 2005. Even before the storm, González watched as more and more of his fellow creative souls were forced to leave the island and seek sustenance on the mainland, gradually whittling down his social circle. With an inquisitive mind that was meticulous and scientific in nature (perhaps his most famous digital work, *Homenaje al*

Cosmos, consisted of a formula where each pixel was created as per a specific mathematical equation), in the years before the storm González grew ever more isolated in his studio-cum-home on Calle Luna, where he nursed an infirm father who eventually died and fought his own battle with liver cancer, perhaps the result of years of heavy drinking. When the storm came, at sixty-seven years old, he was hanging on by a thread, a thread that Maria then snapped in half.

"He had gotten to the age when you hope to continue selling your work and, because of the situation on the island, that just wasn't possible," his friend, the artist Teo Freytes, told me. "He was very depressed and not really taking care of himself, and after the storm the medical system collapsed and he just didn't survive."[450]

A death of neglect under the vise that had been tightening around the island even before the storm, the story of Heriberto González was one that would be written many times on the island in the wake of the tempest.

In the central mountains, the situation was much the same. In Utuado, which had served as the nexus for Pedro Albizu Campos's failed 1950 putsch, Victor Díaz ran a small pharmacy off the town square, the kind of place that served as a hub for local life in the mountain towns of the island.

"We had seen Hurricane Georges [in 1998] and things kept going," he told me as we drove through Utuado's darkened streets one night. "But with Maria, everything stopped. Everything."

The home Diaz shared with his wife, Carmen, was not far from the pharmacy, and boasted a collection of several hundred vinyl LPs of Puerto Rican music that were, miraculously, relatively unscathed. The same could not be said for the wider town and its populace.

"We didn't have electricity for two months, but we had a generator so I was able to start serving people a week after the storm," Díaz told me. "I had to go to San Juan almost every day to get merchandise because no one was bringing it. It was chaos. You had to wait from one day to the other, or go to Arecibo or Manatí, looking for gas. At least five of my customers died in the wake of the storm."

So much had collided to twist the knife into the wound of the island's misery. In Lajas, on the southern coast and an easy morning's drive from Utuado, the first FEMA shipment—two hundred boxes of food and 786 twenty-four packs of water for a town of twenty-five thousand people—arrived more than a week after Maria hit. In the interim, one hundred people, many of them old or infirm, had died in the area during the three days immediately after the storm, twice the typical rate.[451] In March, six months after the hurricane, one hundred thousand people still lacked electricity. Wood and cement poles still teetered dangerously over roads, occasionally falling and killing passerby, as they did with a couple in their sixties in the west of the island that month.[452]

And then there was plain and simple despair.

By early October 2017, a troubling trend had begun to reveal itself. From San Juan to Aguadilla, there appeared to be a marked uptick in suicides, though not yet quite enough to declare a pattern. Men and women, young and old—the anguish appeared not to discriminate.[453] Between November and January, the number of suicides on the island tripled from what it had been the previous year. Between September and December, ninety-six people took their own lives. The emotional distress line of the island's Department of Health had received 1,002 calls from those who were thinking about attempting suicide in December alone, nearly eight hundred more than the previous year.[454] Over a single weekend, a security guard, a policeman, a Justice Department employee, and three others all killed themselves.[455]

As I strolled the central plaza of Guayama several months after the storm, I found it ringing with memorials to the fallen dead. From Puerto Rican soldiers who died fighting in US wars such as World War II and the Korean War, to soldiers from the mainland such as those from Fourth Ohio

Volunteer Infantry "who lost their lives in the performance of their duty in the war with Spain," as the plaque reads, the tributes stood as mute sentinels before the palm-lined square in front of the mayor's office. It was there that I met Rosa Miranda Agosto, a deceptively cheery woman who was the executive director of the Movimiento Evitemos el Suicidio (Let's Avoid Suicide Movement), and we spoke about another kind of war being fought.

"Unfortunately, the way things happened after Hurricane Maria really intensified the incidences of suicide," Miranda Agosto said, referring to the 21 percent increase in people taking their own lives in the wake of the storm and noting that Aguadilla had been particularly hard hit. She was giving out pamphlets on how to recognize signs of suicide and prevent it, and was joined by about fifty other participants also wearing orange T-shirts (the color of suicide prevention and awareness), as well as Guayama's mayor, Eduardo Cintrón, and Puerto Rican senator Evelyn Vázquez.

"The hospital had no electricity at all for fifty-three days," Cintrón, of the pro-commonwealth PPD, told me. "It took us a very long time to even approach any normalcy and, honestly, we are still trying."

A December 2017 data analysis by the *New York Times* suggested the death toll could be as high as 1,052.[456] Following that report, the Rosselló administration announced that it was commissioning a study from George Washington University's Milken Institute School of Public Health to ascertain the full measure of storm-linked mortality.[457] By August 2018, Puerto Rico's government would acknowledge, via a report posted quietly on the website of the Puerto Rico Public–Private Partnerships Authority and without any public fanfare, that it believed the total deaths to be 1,427, more than twenty times the original death toll. The report said that the island's government had known of the increased death count since June.[458] When the report commissioned by the Rosselló administration was finally published that same month, it concluded that the total number of deaths due to Hurricane Maria and its aftermath was 2,975.[459] A study conducted by researchers at the Harvard T.H. Chan School of Public Health and the Beth Israel Deaconess Medical Center and published in the *New England Journal of Medicine* in May 2018 concluded that there were "4,645 excess deaths" between September 20 and December 31, 2017 (a median number between 793 and 8,498 possible deaths during that period), and cautioned that "this number is likely to be an underestimate because of survivor bias,"[460] with people concentrating on those who made it through the tragedy rather than those who had not.

And the US president's response? After the hurricane, whether pursuing a program of separating immigrant families from their children at the US-Mexico border—a policy called "torture" by Amnesty International—[461] attacking the American press by labeling its members, with Stalinesque phrasing, as "enemies of the people";[462] or palling around with North Korea's genocidal dictator Kim Jong-un in Singapore;[463] it was clear his attention was elsewhere, and the lives of the people on the island meant little to him.

Well into 2018, Trump would continue to use false claims to dispute the hurricane's death toll, referencing both Hurricane Maria and Hurricane Irma and claiming on Twitter: "three thousand people did not die in the two hurricanes that hit Puerto Rico. When I left the Island, AFTER the storm had hit, they had anywhere from six to eighteen deaths. As time went by it did not go up by much."[464] He would go on to accuse the death toll as having been "done by the Democrats in order to make me look as bad as possible when I was successfully raising Billions of Dollars to help rebuild Puerto Rico. If a person died for any reason, like old age, just add them onto the list."[465] When Trump's lie elicited the predictable outrage, White House spokesman Hogan Gidley issued a statement railing against "the liberal media and the mayor of San Juan."[466]

In Puerto Rico, the response to Trump's statements was, not surprisingly, one of fury. Leo Cotte, the former mayor of the southern town of Lajas, whose own father had died in the wake of the storm when the oxygen he depended on ran out, said Trump's statements showed "total ignorance of what happened in Puerto Rico during Hurricane Maria" and "a great lack of respect."[467] Rosselló said during an interview with MSNBC that "the victims and the people of Puerto Rico should not have their pain questioned, these are certainly statements that are wrong." Yulín Cruz said the statement showed "a lack of respect for our reality and our pain . . . Three thousand people died on his watch and his inability to grasp that makes him dangerous." On the mainland US, there was also widespread criticism, with Florida's Republican Representative Ileana Ros-Lehtinen asking, "What kind of mind twists that statistic into, 'Oh, fake news is trying to hurt my image?' How can you be so self-centered and try to distort the truth so much? It's mind-boggling."[468]

According to a subsequent study by the London-based journal *BMJ Global Health*, public data demonstrated convincingly that there was a marked disparity in the time it took victims of Hurricane Maria in Puerto Rico to receive assistance as opposed to those on the mainland US—most notably Florida and Texas—who were affected by hurricanes during the same season, one that did "not align with storm severity or prevention and recovery needs." The difference in response created "serious consequences for acute and long-term health and recovery efforts," the journal concluded.[469]

Among such struggle, though, some traditions persisted.

After the storm, Nydia and I were driving east along the coast from San Juan and passed the rolling blue-green surf splashing timelessly on the shore on our left and the beach cabanas and little food shacks of Piñones selling alcapurria fritters on our right. We were heading to Loíza, the bastion of the island's Afro-Caribbean culture. Traversing the swollen Río Grande de Loíza, the words with which the poet Julia de Burgos had memorialized in perhaps her greatest poem came to mind:

¡Río Grande de Loíza!... Río grande. Llanto grande.
El más grande de todos nuestros llantos isleños,
si no fuera más grande el que de mi se sale
por los ojos del alma para mi esclavo pueblo.

(Rio Grande de Loiza!... Great river. Great flood of tears.
The greatest of all our island's tears
save those greater that come from the eyes
up of my soul for my enslaved people.)[470]

Loíza itself was a ramshackle place, low-slung and spread out over several wards. Every year in July, the town held a festival during which it exploded with color, complete with music, distinctive cuisine, and people donning costumes featuring *máscaras de vejigante*—colorful masks based on characters from Puerto Rican folklore. It was in bomba, the music that plantation owners had viewed with such suspicion during slavery times, that Loíza's heart beat the strongest, and I was trying to search out the Ayala family, the genre's foremost proponents on the island.

No amount of cultural ebullience, however, had prepared Loíza for Hurricane Maria. Some three thousand homes, half of its total, were all or partially destroyed during the storm,[471] and the city's electricity grid was leveled. In the weeks and months after the storm, Loíza, whose cultural vibrancy had often been matched by its economic poverty, found itself fighting for survival.

"We're giving food, water, baby food, diapers, and all the necessities that people need here," José Martorell, who worked with La Estrella, a chain of restaurants that delivered *comida criolla*, low-cost Puerto Rican and Cuban food, told me when I found him distributing food to hundreds of people in Loíza's central plaza. Half a dozen Puerto Rican businesses and organizations had organized a distribution of vital items. "In San Juan, we're the fortunate ones that have generators and water, and we needed to give back to the community."[472]

Alongside him was Frankie Colón of the Fundación Caritas Alegres, a nonprofit organization that in normal times provided assistance to children and families with limited resources to meet their health, education, and housing needs.

"We Puerto Ricans are very strong people, but no one was prepared for a hurricane like this," Colón told me. "There is so much to do. It's not going to be a one-week effort. It's going to be years to come of people working together. We can help each other."

Nydia and I found the Ayala family's patriarch, Raúl Ayala, an Afro-Puerto Rican man with close-cropped salt-and-pepper hair and a mustache, in his darkened home. An unseen dog barked incessantly nearby, and he suggested we retire to the family compound to talk, where things might be a little more peaceful.

Ayala's father had been the legendary Cástor Ayala Fuentes, who, in 1959, founded the Ballet Folklórico Hermanos Ayala, the first group to bring the rhythms and dance of bomba to Puerto Rico's television screens on the Telemundo program *Show Time*.

"This is the only town on the island where a majority of residents are of African descent," he told me as we sat in the courtyard of his half-destroyed family home, his sister and a handful of other relatives looking on. The building's roof was gone and water was still pooling on its floors from a recent rain.

"Things are slowly getting better, and we're getting up little by little. But we still have problems. . . . It's imperative to reestablish electricity so things can function. Lots of companies remain closed, and people who don't work don't have salaries, so it's a domino effect."

The walls of the structure still radiated a vivid Caribbean orange and green despite the damage, and there were two small flags, one US and one Puerto Rican, fluttering over the scene of destruction. Ayala told me he felt it was imperative that he and his family carry on their tradition.

"In the cultural life of Puerto Rico," he told me. "Loíza is the town that really represents the African traditions."

As we were getting ready to leave, Nydia began snapping some shots of the family and I and suggested that we pose for one. With all of us standing on the veranda, Ayala, still smiling, reached over and plucked out the American flag from its place so that only the Puerto Rican flag remained.

7

PICKING UP THE PIECES

As Puerto Rico entered its first summer since Hurricane Maria, and with it the beginning of another hurricane season, the dominant narratives on the island appeared to be those of, once again, austerity and profiteering.

At the end of January, FEMA had announced it would "officially shut off" its food and water aid for Puerto Rico, saying that its own analysis demonstrated that only 1 percent of islanders were still relying on assistance. Up to that point it had dispersed $3.2 million in unemployment aid to people whose jobs were affected by the storm and approved—though not dispersed—an additional $500 million in public assistance. In some communities, such as Morovis, where almost the entire town still lacked electricity, up to a third of citizens still depended on the food rations and 51 percent of residents lived below the poverty line.[473] What the economic crisis over the previous years began, Hurricane Maria appeared to accelerate, and US census data would eventually show that Puerto Rico's population declined by 129,848 people—nearly 4 percent of its total population—between July 2017 and July 2018, the largest population drop ever registered on the island.[474]

Around the same time, Rosselló announced that PREPA would be privatized as it had "become a heavy burden for our people, who today are held hostage by its poor service and high cost . . . deficient and obsolete system of generation and distribution of energy is one of the great impediments to our economic development." As PREPA was bankrupt, a judge would have to approve any sale.[475]

As hurricane season loomed, and despite $3.8 billion being spent on the power grid, officials warned that it was "teetering." It been only been partially rebuilt, patched together in piecemeal fashion by crews often working with inadequate supplies, nailing lines to trees in violation of safety codes in a desperate race to electrify the darkened island.[476] One of the contractors recruited to get the grid up and running, a subsidiary of Oklahoma-based Mammoth Energy dubbed Cobra—had been awarded $1.8 billion in federal money and in many cases was charging $4,000 per worker, per day.[477] In March, Walter Higgins, the former CEO of Bermuda-based Ascendant Group Ltd., who had decades of experience in the energy industry, was appointed PREPA's new chief executive officer.[478] The general approval, however, soon turned to rage when it was revealed that Higgins was to be paid $450,000 a year, plus bonuses, with PREPA board chairman Ernesto Sgroi citing a 2016 law that required the utility to pay competitive salaries.[479]

Tired of waiting, in the mountain town of Coamo, residents wielding machetes and shovels began trying to restore the power grid on their own, burrowing holes where they hoped new electrical posts would stand and collecting cables strewn amid the tropical fecundity. In San Sebastian, retired PREPA workers, municipal employees, and other volunteers chipped in.[480] This spirit of resilience was celebrated in one of the more moving responses to the island's state, from New Orleans-based band Hurray For The Riff Raff, whose Bronx-born lead singer and main songwriter Alynda Segarra was of Puerto Rican descent and whose song and video "Pa'lante" powerfully articulated a tradition of struggle, hope, and resistance.

On May 1—May Day—a general strike called by workers and students convulsed the capital, with protesters marching down Ponce de León Avenue, popularly known as the *La Milla de Oro* (Golden Mile), in San Juan's Hato Rey financial district. A day earlier, the FOMB had ratified a doubling of tuition to the Universdad de Puerto Rico, from $56 per credit to $115. Carrying placards assailing the school closings and cuts in education and benefits that had battered the island, the protesters called for a moratorium on pending austerity measures. At the end of the rally, a few dozen protesters clashed with police, leading to latherings of tear gas and thirteen arrests.[481]

After less than four months on the job, Walter Higgins, who had been appointed PREPA's CEO, would resign in early July, citing the furor over his nearly half a million dollar a year compensation as one of the reasons.[482] On the heels of Higgins's departure, Rosselló announced that he was appointing Rafael Diaz-Granados, a member of PREPA's board, as the utility's new CEO. When the disclosure that Diaz-Granados's salary would be $750,000 provoked a storm of criticism (especially from Rosselló, who assailed the board for agreeing to such an arrangement, the new CEO and most of the board quit less than twenty-four hours later. Rosselló then announced that the new CEO would be former PREPA board chairman José Ortiz, who agreed to a $250,000 yearly salary. Ortiz became the fifth PREPA CEO since Maria had hit ten months earlier.[483]

The priority of the FOMB continued to appear to be secrecy, as it refused to comply with local disclosure requirements and tried to avoid sharing with creditors a draft of its fiscal plan and what economic model served as its basis. The FOMB said that creditors sought to exploit any potential discrepancies between drafts of the outlines "in order to mount a challenge to the fiscal plan."[484] In late June, the FOMB announced that it would cut the $25 million scholarship fund from the Universidad de Puerto Rico and a $50 million fund for various municipalities because the island's legislators rejected a change in labor laws that would allow private employers to dismiss workers without cause at any time. Senate president Thomas Rivera Schatz charged, with a touch of hyperbole, that the FOMB threatened to be "worse than Hurricane Maria."[485] In February, the US Court of Appeals for the First Circuit had concluded that the members of the FOMB were "high level federal officials," and thus, the mechanism used to name them violated the Constitution as the appointments had not been sent to the US Senate for approval.[486] The body appealed the ruling.

"We are getting deeper into the colonial relationship. They're not solving that lack of democracy," my friend Juan Ruiz, a thirty-one-year-old who worked in real estate, told me when I visited him in Old San Juan that summer. "Nobody voted for them. It's completely undemocratic."

Many Puerto Ricans had long ago concluded that the FOMB was not working for them, which begged the question: Who *were* they working for?

Shortly after its formation, the FOMB had hired the management consulting firm McKinsey & Company, which began gobbling up nearly a quarter of its budget. By the autumn of 2018, McKinsey would publish a 148-page fiscal plan that advocated even more draconian austerity measures, such as service reductions and job cuts, than had been proposed on the island before. McKinsey itself had by this point billed the board $72 million, and there was plenty of money in its plan going forward: $1.5 billion, to be exact, to be paid to those overseeing the "restructuring"—including, naturally, itself—an amount that would come directly from the Puerto Rican taxpayers the FOMB and its ancillaries were purportedly trying to help.[487] After the island's Centro de Periodismo Investigativo sued the FOMB to obtain its emails with McKinsey, those released revealed that the firm's subsidiary, the McKinsey Investment Office (MIO), directly owned at least $20 million in Puerto Rico bonds through its investments in the hedge fund Whitebox Advisors, and was connected to $170 million more. The blatant conflict of interest of McKinsey advocating a program of brutal austerity that it stood to directly financially benefit from elicited hardly a murmur in Washington.[488]

As the gospel of belt-tightening did not apparently extend to the board itself, the FOMB would go on to sign a $120,000 contract with Washington, DC, consulting firm Fuentes Strategies, a firm with offices in both DC and San Juan, to approach "key" sectors in the United States in order to shape its message before decision makers and the public. Fuentes Strategies would join Williams & Jensen, Off Hill Strategies, and Holland & Knight in lobbying full-time for the junta. By this point, the four firms were being paid over $1.6 million by the FOMB, money which, like that paid to McKinsey, came out of the budget of the government of Puerto Rico.[489]

As chaos roiled PREPA, islanders looking to Puerto Rico's political class for a unified vision forward would be sorely disappointed. At the beginning of July, Rosselló signed into law a version of the island's budget that had been approved by its legislature instead of the one that the FOMB had sought to impose days earlier, which had included $345 million in budget cuts. Promising "to use all the tools I have in my arsenal to be able to defend the people of Puerto Rico," while admitting that the bill signing was likely "a symbolic gesture,"[490] Rosselló, together with the legislature, would subsequently sue the FOMB to avoid implementing the budget.[491] A day later, eighteen of Puerto Rico's twenty-two senators rejected a bill looking to curtail the rights of some workers who had been fired, a move the FOMB had demanded in order to avoid cutting vacation days, sick days, and Christmas bonuses.[492]

In early August, Judge Laura Taylor Swain ruled that the FOMB had the power to make "binding policy choices" over the objections of the island's elected government, but that it had "only budgetary tools and negotiations to use to elicit any necessary buy-in from the elected officials and legislators" in terms of adopting new laws or modifying or repealing existing ones. The decision was a rebuke to Rosselló's attempt to avoid the board-imposed austerity budget, and he responded by charging that the ruling gave "total budgetary authority to the unelected members of the oversight board, which supersede that of the elected officials of the Government of Puerto Rico and its legislature." FOMB Chairman José Carrión called on Rosselló and others to "get back to work" and said the ruling left "no doubt" that the austerity budget "must be enforced."[493]

Nearly a year after the storm, when I drove back into the cordillera central to visit Victor Díaz, the Utuado pharmacist, I found a region still struggling to move on despite the time that had passed. Some life had returned, with coffee shops, small informal bars, and clothing stores doing a brisk trade. But elsewhere, the town's lanes remained lined with shuttered businesses.

"Electricity comes and goes but we never know when," sixty-two-year-old Annie Salva Mercado told me as she stood behind the counter at the bakery she ran near the central square. It was late summer and I had ventured inside to escape a tropical downpour, which had quickly drenched me, only to find my refuge without light, stewing in the humidity. "Things remain very fragile."

In a nearby bodega selling beer, foodstuffs, and candies that children come to purchase after school, a mural of Albizu Campos, his face just above a painted machete, gazed soberly down at patrons. Next to the image were scrawled some words referencing a popular tune by the singer Roy Brown, whose music had become associated with the independentista cause. It read, *aunque naciera en la luna, sigo siendo puertorriqueñ*o. Even though I was born on the moon, I'm still Puerto Rican.

"We have friends and neighbors who still need help," Díaz told me as we drove around the town, examining damaged bridges that remained closed and stoplights that still hadn't begun working again. "We thought FEMA was going to be more proactive with the people of Puerto Rico.

People have been going around begging for help and getting 'no' all the time. Things have not gone back to normal. We are not even at 30 percent after the hurricane."

He was right. At the beginning of April, HUD had announced that Puerto Rico would receive $18.5 billion to help it rebuild its housing, less than the $46 billion Rosselló requested.[494] A year after the hurricane, though insurance companies had paid out a total of $4.4 billion in claims, of the 279,000 total claims for hurricane-related damage, 13,600 claims had still not been closed (by law, insurance companies had ninety days to resolve claims). For the damage that hit Loiza, for example, an insurance company had only paid out $500,000 of a $9 million claim.[495] Survivors also filed some 279,000 claims to insurance companies.[496] By late June, FEMA had approved—but not disbursed—457,000 applications for individual assistance that would total $1.3 billion. And many who did receive assistance complained it was too little, a couple hundred dollars to repair a house that had been rendered almost unlivable.[497]

By September, Rosselló's administration would sue insurance companies it accused of dragging their feet on responding to claims in the hopes that the claims would expire and there would not have to be payouts. The suit said that sixteen thousand claims had not been resolved and demanded $2.6 billion to compensate those who had been affected by the storm.[498] When I drove to Barranquitas to try and talk to FEMA there about what progress had been made, they refused to speak with me, instead issuing a response via email saying that FEMA's response to Hurricane Maria had been "unprecedented" and "the largest and longest federal response to a domestic disaster in the history of the United States."[499]

HUD's inspector general would eventually find that the body had deliberately stonewalled the congressional-mandated investigation into Hurricane Maria-related aid by a policy of "delayed access to departmental records" and a "systemic lack of cooperation," which could cause "oversight efforts to be diluted, become stale, or worse, halt entirely." The Trump

White House, reverting to conspiratorial form, had ordered all government agencies to work closely with it on any oversight or document requests.[500]

Driving through the winding mountain roads of the cordillera central, it was still common to encounter communications poles bent nearly double over the roadside. On some secondary roads, cables and tree branches remained across the path. Many houses seemed abandoned, overlooking sweeping, lush valleys with a sighing melancholy, as if waiting for their owners to return. On one mountainside near Jayuya, I stopped to chat with a pair of PREPA contractors working on an electric pole just off a narrow road. I asked them how the situation was. One, who would only give his name as Javier, summed up the situation using the same word Annie Salva Mercado had in Utuado: fragile.

A year after the storm, another lawsuit filed by the Centro de Periodismo Investigativo forced the government to admit that, contrary to what it had claimed previously for months, it still had no fully completed emergency plan for the island to deal with a Hurricane Maria-scale disaster in the future. After maintaining that the plans had been kept secret for a variety of security concerns, the government conceded that it did not even know when—or if—the plan would be completed.[501] Another major report issued by thirteen federal agencies concluded that Puerto Rico could lose 3.6 percent of its total coastline, eight thousand structures, and drinking water and sanitation pipelines due to climate change–related sea rise. The report also predicted that elevated sea temperatures would increase the intensity of the hurricanes the island would experience.[502]

Lacking any solid disaster response plan, the Rosselló administration instead got into an angry dispute with the Estadísticas de Puerto Rico, the entity tasked with providing the island with independent data. The summer before, the governor had been accused of stacking the institute's board with political cronies, and at the end of 2018, in the eyes of many, he had done much the same again, with three different board members.

The institute filed—then voided—a lawsuit against the governor and suspended its executive director, Mario Marazzi, after it was revealed that his ex-girlfriend had obtained an order of protection against him.[503] Marazzi would eventually resign, charging that "virtually all the members of that illegal board have made political donations and have close economic ties with the government."[504]

The image of an all-blows-allowed fight over government spoils, when so many Puerto Ricans still lacked basic necessities, was dispiriting to watch. In early October, after years of opposition, the island's creditors finally relented and said they would no longer oppose a plan to restructure the circa $4 billion in debt issued by the Government Development Bank, which had been defunct since the previous year. The plan was designed take the bank's portfolio of loans, real estate, and cash and shift it to a debt recovery authority, which would then issue new bonds equal to 55 percent of the outstanding debt.[505] Between June 2017 and June 2018, the island's gross national product had contracted by about 7 percent.[506]

The struggling island had also witnessed the arrival of another kind of investor.

After the storm, a wave of investors and entrepreneurs with links to the cryptocurrency industry and its transaction ledger blockchain arrived in Puerto Rico from the mainland, their most visible representative being Brock Pierce, an eccentric former child actor who became a multimillionaire via the industry. They rented out palatial buildings in Old San Juan, initially using the entire twenty-thousand-square-foot Monastery hotel as their base, and started speaking of how they were going to transform Puerto Rico.[507] Rosselló even established a blockchain advisory council.[508] Pierce, dressed in a leather vest and hat, became a familiar sight wandering around Old San Juan, blasting trance music from a "portable pill-shaped Bluetooth speaker."[509] Even as much of the island lacked power, cruise ships had begun docking in Old San Juan's port the previous December. By the late summer of 2018, the neighborhood was nearly restored to its former glory, even if a number of stores remained closed.

Pierce himself had a somewhat complicated background, to say the least. After appearing in films such as *The Mighty Ducks* as a child actor in the 1990s, Pierce retired from acting at seventeen to eventually cofound, with a businessman in his late thirties named Marc Collins-Rector, a startup called Digital Entertainment Network (DEN), which promised to deliver original video content amid the dot-com boom of the late 1990s. Pierce was a frequent visitor to Collins-Rector's $4.2 million faux-Spanish colonial mansion that had, improbably, once belonged to Death Row Records CEO Suge Knight.[510] Collins-Rector lived there with his twenty-three-year-old boyfriend, Chad Shackley, who had been linked to the investor since he was sixteen. In October 1999, DEN filed for its initial public offering of $75 million, but a month later Collins-Rector settled a suit brought by a man who said he had molested him for years beginning when he was thirteen.[511]

Within months, Collins-Rector was accused of having molested multiple teenage boys and fled to Europe; he was later located and arrested after nearly two years on the run.[512] Other lawsuits would be filed, these naming all three men (Pierce insisted he didn't know about any abuse) and around $4.5 million in judgments were awarded by default.[513] A witness who was a teenager at the time of the alleged abuse said that Pierce "did not take part in this, not at all."[514] By Pierce's own account, he spent most of the next year and a half immersed in the online role-playing game EverQuest.[515] In May 2002, the house in Marbella, Spain, that all three shared was raided and the men were detained (Shackley and Pierce were released without charges). Collins-Rector would finally plead guilty to eight counts of luring teens across state lines for sex, paying only a small fine.[516]

Pierce's subsequent internet venture was Internet Gaming Entertainment (IGE), in which he said Collins-Rector "had no official or unofficial role,"[517] and he would later describe Collins-Rector as "a shit beyond belief."[518] However, the paperwork for the US incorporation of

IGE was filed by Collins-Rector's brother, Matthew Rector, and Collins-Rector's former business partner, attorney Randy Maslow, who at the time also served as IGE's executive vice president.[519] (In 2014, Matthew Rector said he did not know Collins-Rector's whereabouts and hadn't spoken to him in years.[520])

Pierce would later say of this time, "I was dealt a really difficult hand at a young age for not having done anything wrong. Just by association and then, really bad, irresponsible journalism,"[521] and would worry that "anything I accomplish in my life ends up being discredited because of this narrative."[522] Returning to the States and setting about trying to rebuild his life, Pierce crossed paths with none other than Steve Bannon, then a former banker for Goldman Sachs, his career as a cofounder of the bomb-throwing right-wing website Breitbart and chief strategist for the presidential campaign of Donald Trump still in the future. Pierce described Bannon as his "right-hand man" during this time, and Bannon quickly warmed to the avant-garde world of Pierce's cryptocurrency proclivities, saying, "this whole populist revolt is going to come down to this concept of currency." For his part, Pierce described Bannon as "very smart, very driven, very patriotic. He's not most of the things that people say."[523]

Pierce's own interest in Puerto Rico, he said, began while visiting the island as a teenager, and he first started thinking of using the island as a business base around 2014.[524] By the time he landed in San Juan, he was most known for his association with the blockchain company Block.one, which he had sold for some $200 million in EOS virtual currency, and as the director of the Bitcoin Foundation.[525] Many followed him, and despite Pierce's frequent admonitions that they were there to help, the ambitions they voiced often seemed to go beyond mere investing—this new form of arrival seemed reminiscent to some of the old form of colonialism. At one point, Lottery.com cofounder Matt Clemenson told the *New York Times* that the group consisted of "benevolent capitalists," while Pierce said their ethos would be "compassion, respect, financial transparency." In the same article, Blockchain Industries chief technology officer Bryan Larkin declared, "we're going to make this crypto land" as he sipped a frozen piña colada.[526]

Some in Puerto Rico appeared to say "not so fast." When the crypto advocates held a public meeting in Rincón in May 2018, they were met with an often-caustic response on the part of audience members, with Pierce and the others, most of whom could not interact with the audience in Spanish, accused of having "a lack of respect" for the island and its citizens.[527] Attempting to win the audience over to his side by telling them, "It's not about compounding interest, it's about compounding impact," Pierce was at times shouted down and even asked, "Why don't you go to Detroit?" One Bitcoin advocate, relocated from Hawaii, stood up and told the audience, "If this was in place before the hurricane, you wouldn't have to wait for the government to kick in. . . . Now we will be prepared if you allow us to share a new tool, that's all it is. We're not here to take over."[528]

When I spoke to Adam Krim, then acting executive director of the Restart One Foundation, which described itself as a nonprofit organization supporting the redevelopment of Puerto Rico and which was largely seed funded by Pierce, he insisted the new flock of investors came in peace.

"I'm aware that the crypto community came down here without a well-thought-out game plan," Krim told me. "Nonetheless, they came down with the proper intention. We're in the process of building that trust, which is going to take time."

It was not hard to find the anger boiling just below the surface, though. One day, I struck up a conversation with Gabrielle Perez, a twenty-seven-year-old shop assistant in one of the stores selling trinkets to tourists in Old San Juan.

"We are infested with these people who think they are coming to save the primitive people of Puerto Rico who can't get it together," she told me, looking at Calle Fortaleza where Pedro Albizu Campos and Luis Muñoz

Marín both once strolled. "How dare you? It hurts. It's insulting. They want this garden and they see us as the weeds."

But her anger, an anger I heard in many different parts of Puerto Rico, went beyond just the new arrivals and to the government of Puerto Rico itself.

"They're focused on foreign investment, they're focused on tourists, they're focused on everyone but the local community, and I think that's incredibly evident now," she said, speaking in calm, measured tones.

"If it wasn't obvious enough before Maria that we're second-class citizens, now more than ever it's clear where we stand with regard to the United States," Perez continued. "I'm twenty-seven years old and I hope within my lifetime I get to see independence for Puerto Rico. This is a joke. The United States is a superpower, one of the greatest powers in the world, and they can't get the lights on and the water running for a 100-by-33-mile island? What's the point? They can take their citizenship and get out of here. Let us have our island."

Despite Donald Trump's skill at self-promotion and financial sleight of hand, his understanding of global economic matters was often primitive, so when, in late September 2018, he erroneously got the idea into his head that Puerto Rico was using its emergency relief money to pay off its debt, he allegedly lectured White House chief of staff John Kelly and Office of Management and Budget director Mick Mulvaney that no more money should be disbursed to the island. At a meeting several weeks later, Department of Housing and Urban Development deputy secretary Pam Patenaude—who, unlike most administration officials, had visited Puerto Rico at least half a dozen times since the storm—allegedly explained to White House officials that the money had already been appropriated by Congress and could not be withheld or rerouted. She resigned from the administration a few days later.[529]

Beneath the ramparts of Old San Juan, the Caribbean sea splashed onto the shore only feet away from the warren of brightly colored dwellings that were home to the struggling people of La Perla, for whom life trudged on regardless of the dealings of the powers above them. Despite its struggles, the neighborhood, situated on some of the most desirable real estate in the capital and yet housing some of its poorest inhabitants, had become a symbol of the never-say-die spirit of the island. It was memorialized in not only Ismael Rivera's "La Perla" and the video for Luis Fonsi's "Despacito," but also in the song "La Perla" by the Puerto Rican radical group Calle 13, which celebrated the zone's many rough-hewn charms.

It was around dusk one afternoon when the Puerto Rican journalist Joel Cintrón Arbasetti and Old San Juan resident Juan Ruiz-Robles, who had helped run the community kitchen in La Perla in the immediate aftermath of the storm, were sipping ice cold Medalla beers at a makeshift bar in what was once a home, but had now been largely destroyed by the storm. The walls were mostly gone, but the shower in one corner still worked. A local artisan had made a wood carving in the shape of the Puerto Rican flag, through which one could view the tumbling surf as the cruise ship passengers wandered through the streets of the city's colonial gem in the neighborhood above.

"We are in survival mode, here," Antonio Rosario Fernández, a forty-four-year-old salsa bandleader, told me as he relaxed after his day job. "This place was abandoned, with no light, no water, and very little information for a long time and there are still a lot of houses where people can't live."

After our visit to the bar, we wandered through the maze of narrow lanes and found sixty-three-year-old Sonia Viruet, who had lived her whole life in the neighborhood, sitting outside of her humble abode.

"I thought that we would not have the strength to get up again," she told us. "But yes, there was a lot of unity between adults, children, young people, and everyone. The community joined up and the day after Maria, everyone went to collect the rubble, to clean the streets, and to collect wood to try to build some houses."

I asked her if there had been a lot of help from the outside.

"Most of the help we got from private individuals," she said. "From the federal government there was very little, and the mayor didn't even come back to ask us what had happened, who had passed away, what people needed. She hasn't come at all since the storm."

Viruet was echoing a complaint that I had often heard about San Juan mayor Carmen Yulín Cruz, whose office in Old San Juan was only a few blocks away. Despite the respect she had gained for forcefully advocating for Puerto Rico in the wake of the storm and pushing back against Trump's wild slanders, she was increasingly seen as detached and remote, powwowing with Democratic Party grandees on the mainland but virtually absent on the island itself.

A few doors down, fifty-six-year-old Irma Navarez González told much the same tale.

"Many people left during the storm, but I stayed in my house," she told us.

> I was very scared that the sea was going to rise and take me but it was
> my home, so I stayed. . . . When we went out the next morning, the
> streets were filthy, with debris everywhere, but we all made groups,
> in every sector, to start cleaning up. By the night after the storm, we
> had mountains of debris, but the streets were clean. After that, the
> government did not help at all, but we received aid from groups like
> Calle 13—they brought us water and ice—and [the singer] Luis Fonsi
> and [actor] Osvaldo Ríos. Afterward, it seemed like everyone who
> would go to FEMA was told they did not qualify for aid. And the
> people who did—like my neighbors who lost their entire roof, for
> example—were given $300 or $400. And they continue to live life like
> that—with no real roof—even today.

We stayed in the neighborhood late. As stars dappled the night sky, some denizens of La Perla sat in a little park beneath the colonial castle's walls, laughing and talking as the sound of crashing waves echoed nearby, the sweet smell of marijuana drifting on the tropical breeze. Ruiz-Robles and I sat chatting and drinking with a chef who lived in the neighborhood. The strains of salsa and reggaeton weaved through the palm fronds of the moonlit trees.

"This kind of life," he said, as he took in the scene, "this is a kind of resistance."

EPILOGUE

AT THE BEGINNING OF THE TWENTIETH CENTURY, THE PUERTO Rican politician Rosendo Matienzo Cintrón cuttingly commented that "today Puerto Rico is just a crowd. But when the crowd has a soul, then Puerto Rico will be a homeland."[530] Three decades later, in his piercing study of Puerto Rican identity *Insularismo,* Antonio S. Pedreira worried that "our rebellions are momentary, our docility permanent."[531]

Would it always be so?

When Utah Republican Senator Mike Lee introduced a bill to repeal the Jones Act in March 2019, calling it "a huge loss for American consumers and producers" and noting its negative impact on the ability of Puerto Ricans to "rapidly receive the help they need in the wake of natural disasters," the gesture was immediately met with pushback from those with an economic interest in its continuance.[532] At a news conference at the Port of Tampa Bay organized by two industry groups, the Florida Maritime Partnership and the American Maritime Partnership, a few days after the bill's introduction, shipping executives inveighed against any attempt at repeal.

"Without that law, our family-run and employee-owned business and the jobs it has created would not exist," declaimed Kelly Hendry, president of Hendry Marine Industries, one of the linchpins of the area's shipping industry. Representative Charlie Crist, a former Florida governor, also spoke, saying he had a "generally favorable" impression of the Jones Act, which must have come as news to anyone who had spent any time in Puerto Rico recently.[533] As with Blanton Winship, the Koch brothers,

McKinsey & Company, and so many others during the length of Puerto Rico's relationship with the United States, the maritime industry in the United States and the politicians it patronized seemed to see their role as to squeeze a profit—and nothing else—from a prostrate and disempowered island, no matter their own ignorance of its history or the human cost of their endeavors.

Almost at the same time, Donald Trump was bellicosely voicing his opposition to any further aid for Puerto Rico, with Senator Marco Rubio dutifully running interference on the president's behalf.[534] Rubio's colleagues in the Republican-controlled Senate worked to scuttle a relief measure passed by the Democrat-controlled House of Representatives.[535] Amid the debate, Trump claimed that Puerto Rico had received $91 billion in federal recovery funds; more, he claimed, than "any state in the history of the US," when in fact Congress had allocated only $41 billion, far less than the $120 billion that had been allocated after 2005's Hurricane Katrina.[536]

At a public hearing in San Juan organized to help visiting legislators from the mainland get a read on the pulse of islanders' public sentiment toward the mainland, the sense of anguish and frustration was palpable. The hearing was attended by, among others, Arizona Democratic repre- sentative and chairman of the House Committee on Natural Resources Raúl Grijalva, Utah Republican Rob Bishop, and Puerto Rican-American Representatives Nydia Velázquez and Darren Soto (from New York and Florida, respectively). The crowd was dotted with people carrying signs that read "Prosecute bankers," "Cancel the Debt," and "No more PROMESA." One speaker denounced PROMESA as "pure colonialism."[537]

As the Americans bickered, the main hospital on Vieques remained shuttered, with wildlife having taken over its grounds. The closure of the island's only labor and delivery room meant mothers had to travel to the main island to give birth.[538] Nearly two years after the storm, there were still thirty thousand homes with tarpaulin roofs.[539] Many mayors around the island said they still had not been reimbursed by FEMA for the enormous sums of money their municipalities had spent in the wake of the storm.[540] When Trump finally signed a $19 billion disaster relief bill in June 2019, which included additional aid for Puerto Rico as well as for a number of states on the US mainland, he remained churlish, self-obsessed, and petty to the last, tweeting, "Puerto Rico should love President Trump."[541]

At the outset of 2019, Rafael Hernández Colón, who served as governor of Puerto Rico for three terms between 1973 and 1993 for the pro-commonwealth PPD, and who was the last living member of the towering line of Puerto Rican politicians of the previous century, died, bringing what felt, in many ways, like the closing of a chapter. Carmen Yulín Cruz, now the PPD's most prominent politician even though she had continued to be more of a presence in TV studios and at campaign rallies on the mainland United States than among her constituents in San Juan, announced that she would be challenging Ricardo Rosselló for the governorship in 2020. In a speech she declared, "we have to break away from the chains that tie us down in order to have a promising future and break our cycle of poverty." Consciously or not, her words echoed the argument put forth by Luis Muñoz Marín seventy years before, and the fact that the PPD's support for commonwealth status had thus far failed to do what Yulín Cruz again promised was a pregnant subtext.[542]

The Rosselló administration itself was battered by a maelstrom of scandals, many relating to top governmental officals. Following the FBI's May 2019 arrest of the director of the Senate Office of Government Affairs and two contractors for billing for services that were never completed, Rosselló said he "would not tolerate or be an accomplice to any act of corruption."[543] However, in June, Puerto Rico's treasury secretary, Raúl Maldonado, spoke to the WKAQ-580 radio station and announced that he was collaborating with the FBI as the body looked into influence peddling, destruction of documents, and other crimes within the department. Maldonado said the blame fell on an "institutional mafia" within his department composed of "officials who have been with the department for many years," and that he had received death threats and had requested protection from police.[544] His statements appeared to be backed up by comments Douglas Leff, the FBI's special agent in charge on the island, made to *El Nuevo Día* when he said that bribes in the government had occurred in "a dramatic fashion" and that the bureau was pursuing "several investigations at all levels of government."[545]

The day after Maldonado's announcement, I was part of a group of journalists at La Fortaleza. We were ostensibly there to watch Rosselló make an announcement about education. However, when Rosselló strode to the podium, flanked by other government officials and aids, he appeared coiled with rage. Saying that Maldonado had never informed him of the "serious irregularities" that he had made public in his radio interview, and given that the allegations were "grave and could represent serious violations of the law," Rosselló summarily fired Maldonado in front of a stunned press corps, and named Francisco Pares, assistant secretary of internal revenue and tax policy, as acting treasury secretary.[546]

The imbroglio grew even more bizarre from there, as over the next twenty-four hours, Maldonado's son, Raúl Maldonado Nieves, took to Facebook to excoriate Rosselló as "corrupt" and claim that he had personally attended a meeting at the governor's mansion with officials from auditing firm BDO, a company that *El Nuevo Día* had reported was being investigated by the FBI in connection with irregularities connected to its contracts with the territory's government.[547]

Maldonado Nieves said that at the meeting he saw Rosselló order the audit firm to change a report on Hurricane Maria aid and, lapsing into profanity, claimed the report would have shown mismanagement in a relief effort that involved Rosselló's wife, Beatriz. Rosselló responded with an official statement from the governor's office in which he called the allegations "absurd" and "disrespectful." Denying wrongdoing by himself or his wife, he said he wouldn't tolerate attacks on the "integrity of my wife and my family," before going on to speculate that his former treasurer's son must be "going through a moment of personal torment, whatever it may be."[548] The island's secretary of justice, Wanda Vázquez, then summoned the elder Maldonado to appear at her office to explain his allegations. Maldonado ignored her.

Only weeks later, Rosselló's former secretary of education, Julia Keleher; the former head of the commonwealth's Health Insurance Administration; and the managing partner of the auditing firm BDO were among those indicted by the US Justice Department for what the US Department of Education's Office of Inspector General charged was "a public corruption conspiracy" conducted "at the expense of the Puerto Rican public and students."[549]

The Maldonado and Keleher sagas would be overtaken in ensuing days by yet another scandal, when nine hundred pages of chats between Rosselló and his top aides were leaked from the Telegram messaging service. In the chats, the governor and his advisors came off as profane, vengeful, and cruel, mocking his political opponents with often misogynistic and homophobic slurs, openly fantasizing about an assassination of Carmen Yulín Cruz, and heaping ridicule on ordinary Puerto Ricans the government came into contact with. Large demonstrations calling for his resignation made it unclear if his government would survive.

In June 2019, as if to underline how little the fate of the island mattered to those who sought to lead the nation that exercises virtually unfettered power over it, during two days of televised debates among the twenty Democratic candidates seeking to oust Donald Trump from the White House, Puerto Rico was mentioned only once, in passing, when former San Antonio Mayor Julián Castro mentioned that it had been his first campaign stop.[550]

One night I found myself wandering through the streets of Old San Juan. The Iglesia de San José, on which construction had started in 1532 and which had silently watched the dizzying rise and fall of the island's political fortunes, stood solemnly against the night sky as it gazed out on a broad plaza. Along the El Callejón de la Tanca, a *plena* group was playing as patrons downed Medalla beer. Beyond the walls of the old city, reggaeton emanated from the lanes of La Perla, as the Caribbean Sea rolled impassively and anciently on.

As I often do, on the corner of Calle del Sol and Calle de la Cruz, just a few steps from my home, I paused before a lovely pink building. Climbing three stories and with intricate louvered windows and a balcony, the building now houses a French restaurant and two different bars, where tourists, many of them American, can be found ordering drinks in shaky Spanish as international grooves play on the sound system.

The building has another history, though. On the wall outside, a small plaque, which the tourists usually rush by without reading (it's in Spanish), displays a photo of a solemn-faced man with a neatly-trimmed mustache, his arm outstretched, as he addresses an unseen crowd. Translated, the words beneath it read:

> In this building were located the main offices of the Partido
> Nacionalista de Puerto Rico liberation movement and the principal
> residence of the distinguished patriot and independence leader Pedro
> Albizu Campos.

In the shadow-draped lanes of Old San Juan, one still feels the ghosts of Puerto Rico's past, wrestling for exactly what will become of their beloved home, and for a future for the island and its people that remains, as yet, unwritten.

ACRONYMS

EPB Ejército Popular Boricua
FALN Fuerzas Armadas de Liberación Nacional
FEMA Federal Emergency Management Agency
FLT Federación Libre de Trabajadores
FOMB Financial Oversight and Management Board
FRT Federación Regional de Trabajadores
MIRA Movimiento Independentista Revolucionario Armado
MPI Movimiento Pro-Independencia
OVRP Organización de Voluntarios por la Revolución Puertorriqueña
PIP Partido Independentista Puertorriqueño
PNP Partido Nuevo Progresista
PNPR Partido Nacionalista de Puerto Rico
PPD Partido Popular Democrático
PREPA Puerto Rico Electric Power Authority
PROMESA Puerto Rico Oversight, Management, and Economic Stability Act
PS Partido Socialista
PSP Partido Socialista Puertorriqueño
UPR Unión de Puerto Rico

SELECTED BIBLIOGRAPHY

Ayala, César J., and Rafael Bernabe. *Puerto Rico in the American Century: A History Since 1898*. Chapel Hill: University of North Carolina Press, 2007.

Blanco, Tomás. *Prontuario Histórico de Puerto Rico*. San Juan: Ediciones Huracan, 2007.

Brands, H. W., ed. *The Selected Letters of Theodore Roosevelt*. New York: Cooper Square Press, 2001.

de Burgos, Julia. *Song of the Simple Truth: The Complete Poems of Julia de Burgos*. Willimantic: Curbstone Press, 1997.

Denis, Nelson Antonio. *War Against All Puerto Ricans: Revolution and Terror in America's Colony*. New York: Nations Books, 2015.

Díaz, Carmen Graciela. *Huele a bomba: la paradójica esencia del periodismo de Avance*. San Juan: Ediciones Puerto, 2014.

Fernandez, Ronald. *Los Macheteros: The Wells Fargo Robbery and the Violent Struggle for Puerto Rican Independence*. New York: Prentice Hall, 1987.

Figueroa, Luis A. *Sugar, Slavery, and Freedom in Nineteenth-Century Puerto Rico*. Chapel Hill: University of North Carolina Press, 2005.

Fitzpatrick, Joseph P. *Puerto Rican Americans: The Meaning of Migration to the Mainland*. Englewood Cliffs, NJ: Prentice-Hall, 1971.

Gibson, Carrie. *Empire's Crossroads: A New History of the Caribbean*. London: Macmillan, 2014.

Lalo, Eduardo. *Simone: A Novel*. Chicago: University of Chicago Press, 2012.

Lewis, Oscar. *La Vida: A Puerto Rican Family in the Culture of Poverty*. New York: Random House, 1965.

Matos Rodríguez, Félix V. *Women and Urban Change in San Juan, Puerto Rico: 1820–1868*. Gainesville: University Press of Florida, 1999.

Negrón, Luis. *Mundo Cruel: Stories*. New York: Seven Stories Press, 2010.

Nelson, Anne. *Murder Under Two Flags: The U.S., Puerto Rico, and the Cerror Maravilla Cover-Up*. New York: Ticknor & Fields, 1986.

Pedreira, Antonio S. *Insularismo*. Río Piedras: Editorial Edil, 1934.

Piñero, Miguel. *El Bodega Sold Dreams*. Houston, TX: Arte Publico Press, 1985.

Potter, Robert B., and Dennis Conway, eds. *Self-Help Housing, the Poor, and the State in the Caribbean*. Knoxville: University of Tennessee Press, 1997.

Rouse, Irving. *The Tainos: Rise and Decline of the People Who Greeted Columbus*. New Haven: Yale University Press, 1993.

Safa, Helen Icken. *The Urban Poor of Puerto Rico: A Study in Development and Inequality*. New York: Holt, Rinehart & Winston, 1974.

Sánchez, Luis Rafael. *Macho Camacho's Beat*. Champaign, IL: Dalkey Archive Press, 2001.

Sugden, John. *Sir Francis Drake*. New York: Henry Holt & Company, 1990.

Szulc, Tad. *Fidel: A Critical Portrait*. New York: Perennial, 1986.

NOTES

1   Irving Rouse, *The Tainos: Rise and Decline of the People Who Greeted Columbus* (New Haven: Yale University Press, 1993): 5–13.

2   Rouse, *The Tainos*, 154–55.

3   Carrie Gibson, *Empire's Crossroads: A New History of the Caribbean* (London: Macmillan, 2014): 30.

4   Gibson, *Empire's Crossroads*, 43.

5   Rouse, *The Tainos*.

6   Fundación Cultural Educativa Inc., *5 to Centenario de la Rebelión Taína: 1511–2011*, Instituto de Cultura Puertorriqueña, 2011, http://edicionesdigitales.info/biblioteca/rebeliontaina.pdf.

7   Cathy Brian, "Land Tenure Development in Puerto Rico," University of Maine, 2000.

8   Rouse, *The Tainos*.

9   Gibson, *Empire's Crossroads*, 43.

10   Luis A. Figueroa, *Sugar, Slavery, and Freedom in Nineteenth-Century Puerto Rico* (Chapel Hill: University of North Carolina Press, 2005): 31.

11   Figueroa, *Sugar, Slavery, and Freedom*, 180–183.

12   John Sugden, *Sir Francis Drake* (New York: Henry Holt & Company, 1990): 303–308.

13   Sugden, *Sir Francis Drake*, 303–308.

14   Tomás Blanco, *Prontuario Histórico de Puerto Rico* (San Juan: Ediciones Huracan, 1935): 42.

15 Figueroa, *Sugar, Slavery, and Freedom*, 24–25.

16 Blanco, *Prontuario Histórico de Puerto Rico*, 43.

17 Figueroa, *Sugar, Slavery, and Freedom*, 24–25.

18 Ibid.

19 Ibid.

20 Ibid., 10.

21 Ibid., 51.

22 Brian, "Land Tenure Development in Puerto Rico."

23 Blanco, *Prontuario Histórico de Puerto Rico*, 43–44.

24 Nelson Antonio Denis, *War Against All Puerto Ricans: Revolution and Terror in America's Colony* (New York: Nations Books, 2015): 13.

25 Monroe Doctrine of 1823, accessed March 18, 2019, https://www.ourdocuments.gov/doc.php?flash=false&doc=23&page=transcript.

26 Figueroa, *Sugar, Slavery, and Freedom*, 107.

27 Presencia del ideario masónico en el proyecto revolucionario antillano de Ramón Emeterio Betances Oscar G. Dávila del Valle Puertorriqueño. Actualmente es profesor en el Departamento de Humanidades de la Universidad del Sagrado Corazón.

28 César J. Ayala and Rafael Bernabe, *Puerto Rico in the American Century: A History Since 1898* (Chapel Hill: University of North Carolina Press, 2007): 21.

29 Ramón Emeterio Betances, *Diez Mandamientos de los Hombres Libres*.

30 Lola Rodríguez de Tió, "Cuba y Puerto Rico son de un pájaro las dos alas."

31 John Lawrence Tone, *War and Genocide in Cuba 1895–1898* (Chapel Hill: University of North Carolina Press, 2006): 151–224.

32 Figueroa, *Sugar, Slavery, and Freedom*, 107.

33 Bernabé Soto Beltrán, "El movimiento autonomista en Puerto Rico (1887–1898)," *Medium*, September 5, 2014, https://medium.com/@bernabesoto/el-movimiento-autonomista-en-puerto-rico-1887-1898-73f1633b2597.

34 "Los primeros partidos políticos," *Primera Hora*, September 27, 2016, https://www.primerahora.com/noticias/gobierno-politica/nota/losprimerospartidospoliticos-1178013/.

35   Beltrán, "El movimiento autonomista en Puerto Rico (1887–1898)."

36   Ayala and Bernabe, *Puerto Rico in the American Century*, 19.

37   Denis, *War Against All Puerto Ricans*, 13.

38   Marisabel Brás, "The Changing of the Guard: Puerto Rico in 1898," *Hispanic Division of the Library of Congress*, https://www.loc.gov/rr/hispanic/1898/bras.html, accessed April 28, 2019.

39   Blanco, *Prontuario Histórico de Puerto Rico*, 81.

40   H. W. Brands, ed., *The Selected Letters of Theodore Roosevelt*. (New York: Cooper Square Press, 2001): 157.

41   Louis Fisher, "Destruction of the Maine (1898)," *The Law Library of Congress*, August 4, 2009, http://www.loc.gov/law/help/usconlaw/pdf/Maine.1898.pdf.

42   William McKinley, "War Message," April 11, 1898.

43   The Teller Amendment, April 20, 1898.

44   Anne Nelson, *Murder Under Two Flags: The U.S., Puerto Rico, and the Cerro Maravilla Cover-Up* (New York: Ticknor & Fields, 1986): 30.

45   Ayala and Bernabe, *Puerto Rico in the American Century*, 29.

46   Editorial, *New York Times*, July 11, 1898.

47   Denis, *War Against All Puerto Ricans*, 13–14.

48   "Puerto Rico at the Dawn of the Modern Age: Late- Nineteeth and Early-Twentieth-Century Perspectives," History, The Library of Congress, https://www.loc.gov/teachers/classroommaterials/connections/puerto-rico/history3.html.

49   John A. Gable, Letter to the Editor, "Credit 'Splendid Little War,' to John Hay" *New York Times*, July 9, 1991.

50   The authoritative accounts of this period can be found in the works of Haitian historian Roger Gaillard.

51   Stuart B. Schwartz, "The Hurricane of San Ciriaco: Disaster, Politics, and Society in Puerto Rico, 1899–1901," *Hispanic American Historical Review* 72, no. 3 (August 1992): 303–334.

52   Ibid.

53   Ayala and Bernabe, *Puerto Rico in the American Century*, 54–55.

54 Ibid., 17.

55 Ibid., 61–62.

56 Ibid., 62.

57 Gen. George W. Davis, "Report of the military governor of Porto Rico on civil affairs," United States, Division of Insular Affairs, 1902, https://archive.org/details/reportofmilitary00puer, accessed January 2, 2019.

58 Charles Herbert Allen, "First Annual Report of Charles H. Allen, Governor of Porto Rico, Covering the Period from May 1, 1900 to May 1, 1901" Fundación Puertorriqueña de las Humanidades, Academia Puertorriqueña de la Historia, 2005.

59 Denis, *War Against All Puerto Ricans*, 58.

60 *Foraker Act (Organic Act of 1900)*, 56th Cong., 1st sess., *U.S. Statutes at Large* (1900): 77–86.

61 Transcript of Platt Amendment (1903).

62 Kate Connolly, "German archive reveals Kaiser's plan to invade America," *The Guardian*, May 8, 2002, https://www.theguardian.com/world/2002/may/09/kateconnolly.

63 Theodore Roosevelt's Annual Message to Congress, December 6, 1904.

64 Speech of Luis Muñoz Rivera in favor of the Jones Bill on the floor of the US House of Representatives, May 5, 1916.

65 Denis, *War Against All Puerto Ricans,* 80.

66 Ibid., 59–60.

67 Ibid., 110–115.

68 *Balzac v. Porto Rico, 258 U.S. 298* (1922).

69 Denis, *War Against All Puerto Ricans,* 115.

70 Ayala and Bernabe, *Puerto Rico in the American Century,* 109.

71 Ibid., 180.

72 Ibid., 41–42.

73 Ibid., 33.

74 Ibid., 33.

75 Ibid., 96.

76 Helen Icken Safa, *The Urban Poor of Puerto Rico: A Study in Development and Inequality* (New York: Holt, Rinehart & Winston, 1974): 2.

77 Kathryn Krase, "History of Forced Sterilization and Current U.S. Abuses," *Our Bodies Our Selves*, October 1, 2014, https://www.ourbodiesourselves.org/book-excerpts/health-article/forced-sterilization/, accessed February 4, 2019.

78 Dr. Helen Rodriguez-Trias bio, National Institutes of Health, https://cfmedicine.nlm.nih.gov/video/273_1_trans.html, accessed February 4, 2019.

79 Denis, 90–93. The poetry gene evidently ran in the family, as Muñoz Marín's cousin, Mercedes Negrón Muñoz, was also an accomplished poet.

80 Luis Muñoz Marín, "The Sad Case of Puerto Rico," *American Mercury* XVI, no. 62 (February 1929).

81 Joanne Omang, "Luis Munoz Marin, 4-Term Governor of Puerto Rico, Dies," *Washington Post*, May 1, 1980, https://www.washingtonpost.com/archive/local/1980/05/01/luis-munoz-marin-4-term-governor-of-puerto-rico-dies/06ecd114-edb1-4908-98ab-4de668ee3f2d/?noredirect=on&utm_term=.56168e7f52f8.

82 Mireya Navarro, "New Light on Old F.B.I. Fight; Decades of Surveillance of Puerto Rican Groups," *New York Times*, November 28, 2003.

83 Denis, *War Against All Puerto Ricans,* 87–98.

84 Ayala and Bernabe, *Puerto Rico in the American Century,* 96–97.

85 Denis, *War Against All Puerto Ricans,* 43.

86 Ibid., 116–17.

87 Ibid., 118–20. Albizu Campos was now firmly in the sights of both the local and national security apparatus, and his FBI file would eventually grow to forty-seven hundred pages.

88 Ibid., 66–70.

89 "Legislative Interests: Committee Assignments," History, Art & Archives, US House of Representatives, https://history.house.gov/Exhibitions-and-Publications/HAIC/Historical-Essays/Foreign-Domestic/Legislative-Interests/, accessed February 10, 2019.

90 Denis, *War Against All Puerto Ricans,* 122.

91 Ibid., 43–54.

92 Vito Marcantonio speech to US Congress, August 14, 1939.

93   Denis, *War Against All Puerto Ricans,* 71.

94   "The Puerto Rican Economy: Historical Perspectives and Current Challenges," Fundación Luis Muñoz Marín, March 13, 2017.

95   Joseph Fitzpatrick, *Puerto Rican Americans: The Meaning of Migration to the Mainland* (Englewood Cliffs, NJ: Prentice-Hall, 1971): 16.

96   Molly Crabapple, "The Fatal Conscience: Julia de Burgos, Puerto Rico's Greatest Poet," *New York Review of Books*, April 26, 2018. This essay is an excellent brief summary of de Burgos's life and career.

97   Julia de Burgos, *Song of the Simple Truth: The Complete Poems of Julia de Burgos* (Willimantic, CT: Curbstone Press, 1997).

98   Ayala and Bernabe, *Puerto Rico in the American Century*, 142.

99   Charles R. Venator-Santiago, "Are Puerto Ricans Really American Citizens?" *The Conversation*, March 2, 2017, http://theconversation.com/are-puerto-ricans-really-american-citizens-73723.

100   "Operation Bootstrap," http://lcw.lehman.edu/lehman/depts/latinampuertori-can/latinoweb/PuertoRico/Bootstrap.htm, accessed April 24, 2019.

101   Juan Ruiz Toro, "Puerto Rico's Operation Bootstrap," Modern Latin America, Brown University Library, Center for Digital Scholarship, https://library.brown.edu/create/modernlatinamerica/chapters/chapter-12-strategies-for-econom-ic-developmen/puerto-ricos-operation-bootstrap/, accessed April 24, 2019.

102   In many aspects, the Ley de la Mordaza appeared based on the Alien Registration Act, more widely known as the Smith Act, enacted on the continental United States eight years earlier.

103   Text of Law 53.

104   Denis, *War Against All Puerto Ricans*, 193.

105   Ibid., 193–196.

106   Ibid., 196–200.

107   Ibid., 201–202.

108   Ibid., 3–9.

109   "No One Expected Attack on Congress in 1954," Associated Press, February 29, 2004.

110   Denis, *War Against All Puerto Ricans,* 234–238.

111 Molly Crabapple, "The Fatal Conscience."

112 Vanessa Perez, "Celebrating 99 years of Julia de Burgos," *Huffington Post*, May 4, 2013, https://www.huffpost.com/entry/julia-de-burgos_b_2703750.

113 Safa, *The Urban Poor of Puerto Rico*, 21.

114 Ayala and Bernabe, *Puerto Rico in the American Century*, 190.

115 Ibid., 181.

116 Safa, *The Urban Poor of Puerto Rico*, 1–11.

117 Michael Deibert, "San Juan's Iconic La Perla Neighborhood Defies Trump," *Daily Beast*, September 17, 2018.

118 Joseph P. Fitzpatrick, *Puerto Rican Americans: The Meaning of Migration to the Mainland* (Englewood Cliffs, NJ: Prentice-Hall, 1971): 48.

119 Safa, *The Urban Poor of Puerto Rico*, 1.

120 Ayala and Bernabe, *Puerto Rico in the American Century*, 184.

121 Fitzpatrick, *Puerto Rican Americans*, 10.

122 Navarro, "New Light on Old FBI Fight."

123 Ibid.

124 José Javier Colón Morera, "Las carpetas de Juan Mari Brás" (Presentation, La Conferencia de la Celebración del Nacimiento de Juan Mari Brás, December 2, 2013).

125 Leonard Bernstein and Stephen Sondheim, "America," *West Side Story*, 1957.

126 Safa, *The Urban Poor of Puerto Rico*, 33.

127 "President John F. Kennedy's Remarks at Isla Verde Int. Airport, San Juan," https://www.dailymotion.com/video/x2w0xxv, accessed September 21, 2018.

128 Tad Szulc, *Fidel: A Critical Portrait* (New York: Perennial, 1986): 195–333.

129 Safa, *The Urban Poor of Puerto Rico*, 100.

130 Omang, "Luis Muñoz Marín, 4-Term Governor of Puerto Rico, Dies."

131 Michelle Samuels, "Puerto Rico Shows Harm of Medicaid Caps," Boston University School of Public Health, November 21, 2017, http://www.bu.edu/sph/2017/11/21/puerto-rico-shows-harm-of-medicaid-caps/.

132 Ian James, "Former Puerto Rican Gov Luis Ferré Dies," Associated Press, October 21, 2003.

133 Edmund H. Mahoney, "Revolutionary to the End," *Hartford Courant*, November 20, 2005, https://www.courant.com/news/connecticut/hc-xpm-2005-11-20-0511200623-story.html.

134 Edmund H. Mahoney, "The Untold Tale of Victor Gerena," *Hartford Courant*, November 7, 1999, https://www.courant.com/news/connecticut/hc-xpm-1999-11-07-9911060427-story.html.

135 Ana Nadal Quiros, "Filiberto Ojeda Ríos, el 'Che Guevara' de Puerto Rico," *El Mundo*, September 27, 2005, https://www.elmundo.es/elmundo/2005/09/27/obituarios/1127801993.html.

136 Héctor Meléndez, "El Partido Socialista en los años 70," *80 grados*, July 15, 2016.

137 Gloria Ruiz Kuilan, "Hoy se Cumplen 45 años del Asesinato de Antonia Martínez Lagares," *El Nuevo Día*, March 4, 2015.

138 Nelson, *Murder Under Two Flags,* 103.

139 Nelson, *Murder Under Two Flags*, 105–106.

140 Ibid,, 116.

141 Ibid., 118.

142 Ibid., 10.

143 Abbie Boudreau and Scott Bronstein, "Island residents sue U.S., saying military made them sick," *CNN Special Investigations Unit*, February 1, 2010.

144 Valeria Pelet, "Puerto Rico's Invisible Health Crisis," *The Atlantic*, September 3, 2016.

145 "Puerto Ricans Vow to Avenge Death in US Prison," *New York Times*, November 18, 1979.

146 "Puerto Ricans Vow to Avenge Death," *New York Times*.

147 Tom Wicker, "Coming Home Election," *New York Times*, February 11, 1973.

148 Ayala and Bernabe, *Puerto Rico in the American Century*, 232–233.

149 John Van Hyning, "Confronting an Island's Ills," *Washington Post*, January 2, 1977.

150 Leonard Silk, "Puerto Rico Swallows Its Bitter Economic Medicine," *New York Times*, July 18, 1976.

151 Ibid.

152 Ibid.

153 Quiros, "Filiberto Ojeda Ríos, el 'Che Guevara' de Puerto Rico."

154 Rose Davis and Larry McShane, "Ex-cop who lost eye in NYC FALN blast slams pick of Oscar Lopez Rivera as Puerto Rican Day Parade honoree," *New York Daily News*, May 27, 2017, https://www.nydailynews.com/new-york/lopez-rivera-no-hero-ex-cop-lost-eye-nyc-faln-blast-article-1.3201191.

155 "Puerto Rico Bomb Kills 2, Injures 11," *New York Times*, January 13, 1975.

156 Mara Bovsun, "FALN Bomb Kills 4 at Fraunces Tavern, Where George Washington Said Farewell to Troops," *New York Daily News*, January 21, 2012, https://www.nydailynews.com/new-york/faln-bomb-kills-4-fraunces-tavern-article-1.1008711.

157 "Terroristic Activity: The Cuban Connection in Puerto Rico," http://www.latinamericanstudies.org/terrorism/cuban-connection-pr-1.htm, accessed June 2019.

158 Szulc, *Fidel: A Critical Portrait*, 641.

159 Carlos Romero Barceló, "Puerto Rico, U.S.A: The Case for Statehood," *Foreign Affairs* 59, no. 1 (Fall 1980): 60–81.

160 Van Hyning, "Confronting an Island's Ills."

161 Miguel Piñero, *El Bodega Sold Dreams* (Houston, TX: Arte Publico Press, 1985): 8.

162 "Consul's Abductors Give Up in San Juan," *New York Times*, July 5, 1978.

163 Nelson, *Murder Under Two Flags*, 146–147.

164 Nelson, *Murder Under Two Flags*, 139–40.

165 Ibid., 133–36.

166 Ibid., 148–49.

167 Ibid., 162–166.

168 Ibid., 197.

169 "Puerto Ricans Were Kneeling When Killed by Police, Officer Says," *New York Times*, November 30, 1983, https://www.nytimes.com/1983/11/30/us/puerto-ricans-were-kneeling-when-killed-by-police-officer-says.html.

170 Manuel Suarez, "Ex-Police Official Acquitted in Two Puerto Rico Killings," *New York Times*, March 18, 1988, https://www.nytimes.com/1988/03/18/us/ex-police-official-acquitted-in-two-puerto-rico-killings.html.

171 Mireya Navarro, "Puerto Rico Gripped by Its Watergate," *New York Times*, January 30, 1992, https://www.nytimes.com/1992/01/30/us/puerto-rico-gripped-by-its-watergate.html.

172 "Police Agent in Puerto Rico Deaths is Assassinated," *New York Times*, May 1, 1986, https://www.nytimes.com/1986/05/01/us/police-agent-in-puerto-rico-deaths-is-assassinated.html.

173 Ejército Popular Boricua, "Mensaje al pueblo," October 30, 1978.

174 Clyde Haberman, "Terrorists in Puerto Rico Ambush Navy Bus, Killing 2 and Injuring 10," *New York Times*, December 4, 1979, https://www.nytimes.com/1979/12/04/archives/terrorists-in-puerto-rico-ambush-navy-bus-killing-2-and-injuring-10.html.

175 Ejército Popular Boricua, "Acción contra la Base Naval de Inteligencia," December 3, 1979.

176 Mayra Montero, "Magic and Realism," *New York Times*, November 30, 2004, https://www.nytimes.com/2004/11/30/opinion/magic-and-realism.html.

177 US Congress, *Omnibus Budget Reconciliation Act of 1981*, HR 3982, 97th Cong., introduced in House June 19, 1981, https://www.congress.gov/bill/97th-congress/house-bill/3982/summary/00.

178 Joseph B. Treaster, "Head of Reagan panel apologizes to Puerto Ricans," *New York Times*, May 29, 1982, https://www.nytimes.com/1982/05/29/us/head-of-reagan-panel-apologizes-to-puerto-ricans.html.

179 Harold Lidin, "Terrorists in Puerto Rico Destroy Guard Jets," *Washington Post*, January 13, 1981.

180 Ejército Popular Boricua, "Operativo militar Pitirre II," January 13, 1981.

181 Robert B. Potter and Dennis Conway, eds., *Self-Help Housing, the Poor, and the State in the Caribbean* (Knoxville: University of Tennessee Press, 1997): 25.

182 Jo Thomas, "Puerto Rico Terrorist Group Takes Responsibility for Blackout," *New York Times*, November 29, 1981, https://www.nytimes.com/1981/11/29/us/puerto-rico-terrorist-group-takes-responsibility-for-blackout.html.

183 "Squatters Occupy Capitol," UPI, May 19, 1982, https://www.upi.com/Archives/1982/05/19/Squatters-occupy-Capitol/7823003990687/.

184 Armando André, "Terrorismo en Puerto Rico: 1979–1982," *La Crónica Gráfica*, 1987.

185 For the definitive account of the robbery, see Ronald Fernandez, *Los Macheteros: The Wells Fargo Robbery and the Violent Struggle for Puerto Rican Independence* (New York: Prentice Hall, 1987).

186 Mahoney, "The Untold Tale of Victor Gerena."

187 Armando André, "Terrorismo en Puerto Rico: Los Macheteros se Delatan Unos a Otros," *La Crónica Gráfica*, 1987.

188 "12 'Terrorists' Held in Heist of $7 Million," *United Press International*, August 30, 1985.

189 André, "Terrorismo en Puerto Rico."

190 "Florida Arrests 2,100 in Crack Roundup," *Los Angeles Times*, August 27, 1989.

191 Rafael Hernandez Colon, "Statehood for Puerto Ricans," *New York Times*, February 26, 1990, https://www.nytimes.com/1990/02/26/opinion/state-hood-for-puerto-ricans.html.

192 Ferdinand Quinones and Karl G. Johnson, *The Floods of May 17–18, 1985 and October 6–7, 1985 in Puerto Rico, United States Geological Survey*, (San Juan, PR: US Department of the Interior, 1987).

193 Ayala and Bernabe, *Puerto Rico in the American Century*, 292.

194 Stephen Smith, "Puerto Rican Fugitive Killed," Associated Press, September 24, 2005.

195 Rebecca Spalding and Jonathan Levin, "Puerto Rico's Governor Has to Clean Up His Dad's Mess," *Bloomberg*, April 19, 2017, https://www.bloomberg.com/news/articles/2017-04-19/his-father-ran-up-puerto-rico-s-debt-he-now-has-to-fix-the-mess.

196 Larry Rohter, "Puerto Rico Fighting to Keep Its Tax Breaks for Businesses," *New York Times*, May 10, 1993, https://www.nytimes.com/1993/05/10/business/puerto-rico-fighting-to-keep-its-tax-breaks-for-businesses.html.

197 Dan Burton and Peter Deutsch, "It's Time to Reform the Puerto Rico Tax Credit," *Christian Science Monitor*, January 16, 1996.

198 Rohter, "Puerto Rico Fighting to Keep Its Tax Breaks for Businesses."

199 Ibid.

200 Larry Luxner, "US Law Change Shakes Island," The JOC Group, December 9, 1996.

201 Luxner, "US Law Change Shakes Island."

202 Tristan Clavel, "Trafficking Routes Up for Grabs After Fall of Top Caribbean Drug Kingpin," Insight Crime, August 17, 2017, https://www.insightcrime.org/news/analysis/trafficking-routes-up-for-grabs-after-fall-top-caribbean-drug-kingpin/.

203 "Golpe en La Perla," *Primera Hora*, June 30, 2011, https://www.primerahora.com/noticias/policia-tribunales/nota/golpeenlaperla-520904/.

204 Ben Fox, "Raid Opens Window into Notorious Puerto Rico Slum," Associated Press, June 30, 2011.

205 "Puerto Ricans Say 'No' to Statehood," CNN, December 14, 1998, http://www.cnn.com/WORLD/americas/9812/14/puerto.rico.01/.

206 Danica Coto, "Puerto Rico Unveils 1st Balanced Budget in Years," Associated Press, April 30, 2014.

207 Sergio M. Marxuach, *The Puerto Rican Economy: Historical Perspectives and Current Challenges*, Fundación Luis Muñoz Marín, Center for the New Economy, March 13, 2017, http://grupocne.org/wp-content/uploads/2012/02/FLMM.pdf.

208 Spalding and Levin, "Puerto Rico's Governor Has to Clean Up His Dad's Mess."

209 John Marino, "U.S. Corruption Prosecutions Rock Puerto Rico," *Washington Post*, August 27, 2000, https://www.washingtonpost.com/archive/politics/2000/08/27/us-corruption-prosecutions-rock-puerto-rico/12e0ec42-e7b8-4cb1-aed4-090a3a78e1da/.

210 "Puerto Rico Officials Charged with Corruption," Associated Press, January 23, 2002, https://www.nytimes.com/2002/01/23/national/puerto-rico-officials-charged-with-corruption.html.

211 Mireya Navarro, "Puerto Rico Journal; It's Good Talk, but Bad Language," *New York Times*, January 30, 2002, https://www.nytimes.com/2002/01/30/us/puerto-rico-journal-it-s-good-talk-but-bad-language.html.

212 John Marino, "Puerto Rico's New War on Poverty," *Washington Post*, September 4, 2002.

213 Marxuach, *The Puerto Rican Economy: Historical Perspectives and Current Challenges*.

214 "Navy Attributes Fatal Bombing to Mistakes," Associated Press, August 3, 1999.

215 Edward Walsh, "U.S. Navy Bombs, Shells Rain on Vieques Island as Protests Continue," *Washington Post*, April 28, 2001, https://www.washingtonpost.com/archive/politics/2001/04/28/us-navy-bombs-shells-rain-on-vieques-island-as-protests-continue/5d435025-208a-409c-a4a1-0db14f8da5a1/.

216 Mike Clary, "Vieques Protesters Removed Without Incident," *Los Angeles Times*, May 5, 2000, https://www.latimes.com/archives/la-xpm-2000-may-05-mn-26735-story.html.

217 Walsh, "U.S. Navy Bombs, Shells Rain on Vieques Island as Protests Continue."

218 Yves Colon, "Puerto Rico's New Governor Inspires Hope," *Miami Herald*, February 4, 2001.

219 John Thor Dahlberg, "Vieques Bombing Resumes Amid Violent Protests," *Los Angeles Times*, April 28, 2001.

220 Kate Snow and Kelly Wallace, "Bush says Navy will quit bombing Vieques," CNN, June 14, 2001.

221 Dana Canedy, "Navy Leaves a Battered Island, and Puerto Ricans Cheer," *New York Times*, May 2, 2003, https://www.nytimes.com/2003/05/02/us/navy-leaves-a-battered-island-and-puerto-ricans-cheer.html.

222 Valeria Pelet, "Puerto Rico's Invisible Health Crisis."

223 Ejército Popular Boricua, "Con motivo del 102 Aniversario de la Invasión Yanqui," July 25, 2000.

224 Texto íntegro de la entrevista a Filiberto Ojeda Ríos realizada por José Elías Torres, Director de Noticias de WPAB, y que fue al aire en agosto de 2005. Trascripción de CLARIDAD.

225 "Execution of Federal Arrest Warrant," US Department of Justice, September 24, 2005.

226 Abby Goodnough, "Killing of Militant Raises Ire in Puerto Rico," *New York Times*, September 28, 2005.

227 Ibid.

228 Ibid.

229 "Puerto Rico Sues U.S. Over Slaying of Militant," *Miami Herald*, March 24, 2006.

230 "Court Refuses to Step into Ojeda Case," Associated Press, March 31, 2008.

231 Edmund Mahoney, "Revolutionary to the End."

232 Miranda Leitsinger, "Puerto Rico Days Away from Government Shutdown, Leader Warns," Associated Press, April 27, 2006.

233 "Loan Deal for Puerto Rico Crisis," BBC, May 11, 2006, http://news.bbc. co.uk/2/hi/americas/4760411.stm.

234 "New Puerto Rico Gov Faces Soaring Crime, Deficit," Associated Press, January 2, 2009.

235 Kirk Semple, "U.S. Issues Indictment of Governor in Puerto Rico," *New York Times*, March 28, 2008, https://www.nytimes.com/2008/03/28/us/28puerto. html.

236 "Puerto Rico Ex-Governor Cleared in Corruption Trial," Associated Press, March 20, 2009.

237 "New Puerto Rico Gov Faces Soaring Crime, Deficit," Associated Press.

238 Ben Fox, "Puerto Rico Ups Holiday Patrols After Deadly Year," Associated Press, December 31, 2008.

239 "U.S. Struggles to Keep Up in Puerto Rico's Drug War," Associated Press, September 21, 2009.

240 "Puerto Rico police investigate killings of 3 teens," Associated Press, September 30, 2009.

241 "7 killed, 20 injured in Puerto Rico bar shooting," Associated Press, October 18, 2009.

242 "United States of America, Appellee, v. Alexis Candelario–Santana, and David Oquendo–Rivas, Defendants, Appellants. Nos. 13–2139, 13–2427," https:// caselaw.findlaw.com/us-1st-circuit/1746360.html, accessed September 22, 2018.

243 AJ Vicens, "You've Probably Never Heard of America's Worst Police Force," *Mother Jones*, February 27, 2015, https://www.motherjones.com/politics/ 2015/02/puerto-rico-police-department-abuses-reform/.

244 American Civil Liberties Union, *Island of Impunity: Puerto Rico's Outlaw Police Force*, June 2012, https://www.aclu.org/report/island-impunity-puerto-ricos -outlaw-police-force.

245 "New Puerto Rico Gov Faces Soaring Crime, Deficit," Associated Press.

246 "Puerto Rico Union Leaders Clash with Police," Associated Press, September 29, 2009.

247 Patrick Brennan, "Puerto Rico: A Latin Liechtenstein?" *National Review*, March 15, 2013, https://www.nationalreview.com/corner/puerto-rico-latin -liechtenstein-patrick-brennan/.

248 Danica Coto, "Puerto Rico police chief quits amid crime concerns," Associated Press, July 2, 2011.

249 "Golpe en La Perla," *Primera Hora*.

250 Antonio R. Gomez, "Sentencian a 30 Años de Cárcel a Líder Comunitario de La Perla," *Primera Hora*, July 30, 2014, https://www.primerahora.com/noticias/ policia-tribunales/nota/sentenciana30anosdecarcelalidercomunitariodelaperla -1025611/.

251 Ben Fox, "Raid Opens Window into Notorious Puerto Rico Slum," Associated Press, June 30, 2011.

252 Danica Coto, "Santero Priest Targeted in Puerto Rico Drug Operation," Associated Press, April 3, 2012.

253 "Puerto Rico Bank Executive Slain on Busy Highway," Associated Press, June 16, 2011.

254 Zeke Faux, "The Strange Story of a Murdered Banker in Puerto Rico," *Bloomberg*, July 6, 2016, https://www.bloomberg.com/features/2016-doral-bank-murder/.

255 Danica Coto, "6 Charged in '11 Killing of US Bank Executive in Puerto Rico," Associated Press, December 12, 2018.

256 Coto, "Puerto Rico Police Chief Quits Amid Crime Concerns."

257 Danica Coto, "32 homicides in 11 days: Puerto Rico fears murder surge after Hurricane Maria," Associated Press, January 11, 2018.

258 "Puerto Rico's Police Chief Quits Amid Crime Spike," Associated Press, March 28, 2012.

259 Bruce Weber, "Hector Camacho, 50, Boxer Who Lived Dangerously, Dies," *New York Times*, November 24, 2012.

260 "End Nears for Shot Boxer Hector 'Macho' Camacho," Associated Press, November 24, 2012.

261 "Cadáver Encontrado en Guavate es de Publicista Desaparecido," *Primera Hora,* December 3, 2012, https://www.primerahora.com/noticias/policia-tribunales/ nota/cadaverencontradoenguavateesdepublicistadesaparecido-730689/.

262 Mariana Cobián, "Diecinueve años de prisión a último coacusado en caso del asesinato del publicista," *Primera Hora*, June 17, 2015, https://www.primera-hora.com/noticias/policia-tribunales/nota/diecinueveanosdeprisionaultimocoa-cusadoencasodelasesinatodelpublicista-1089608/.

263 Zuania Ramos, "Puerto Rico Murder Sparks Social Media Campaign Seeking Peace: #TodosSomosJoséEnrique," *Huffington Post*, December 5, 2012.

264 "Puerto Ricans Opt for Statehood in Referendum," Associated Press, November 7, 2012.

265 Ben Fox and Danica Coto, "Puerto Rico Ousts Governor, Backs US Statehood," Associated Press, November 8, 2012.

266 Coto, "Puerto Rico Unveils 1st Balanced Budget in Years."

267 Danica Coto, "Life in Puerto Rico Becomes Costlier Amid Crisis," Associated Press, September 29, 2013.

268 Jonathan Mahler and Nicholas Confessore, "Inside the Billion-Dollar Battle for Puerto Rico's Future," *New York Times*, December 19, 2015, https://www.nytimes.com/2015/12/20/us/politics/puerto-rico-money-debt.html.

269 Mary Williams Walsh, "Worsening Debt Crisis Threatens Puerto Rico," *New York Times*, October 7, 2013, https://dealbook.nytimes.com/2013/10/07/worsening-debt-crisis-threatens-puerto-rico/.

270 Jaison Abel, et al., *An Update on the Competitiveness of Puerto Rico's Economy* (New York: Federal Reserve Bank of New York, July 31, 2014).

271 Diane Brady, "Puerto Rico's Governor Pitches a Story of Progress for His Troubled Island," *Bloomberg Businessweek*, April 9, 2014, https://www.bloomberg.com/news/articles/2014-04-09/puerto-ricos-governor-pitches-a-story-of-progress-for-his-troubled-island.

272 United States Government Accountability Office, *Puerto Rico: Information on How Statehood Would Potentially Affect Selected Federal Programs and Revenue Sources*, March 2014, https://www.gao.gov/assets/670/661334.pdf.

273 Mary Williams Walsh, "S.&P. Lowers Puerto Rico Debt to Junk Status," *New York Times*, February 4, 2014, https://dealbook.nytimes.com/2014/02/04/s-p-lowers-puerto-rico-debt-to-junk-status/.

274 Michael Corkery, "Investors Appear to Shrug Off Puerto Rico's Debt Downgrade," *New York Times*, February 5, 2014, https://dealbook.nytimes.com/2014/02/05/investors-appear-to-shrug-off-puerto-ricos-debt-downgrade/.

275 Mary Williams Walsh and Michael Corkery, "Puerto Rico Wants to Incur More Debt to Regain Financial Footing," *New York Times*, February 18, 2014, https://dealbook.nytimes.com/2014/02/18/puerto-rico-wants-to-incur-more-debt-to-regain-financial-footing/.

276 Michael Corkery, "Puerto Rico Hires Bankruptcy Lawyers," *New York Times*, April 7, 2014, https://dealbook.nytimes.com/2014/04/07/puerto-rico-hires-bankruptcy-lawyers/.

277 Walsh and Corkery, "Puerto Rico Wants to Incur More Debt to Regain Financial Footing."

278 Brady, "Puerto Rico's Governor Pitches a Story."

279 Coto, "Puerto Rico Unveils Budget."

280 Ibid.

281 Katherine Burton, "John Paulson Calls Puerto Rico Singapore of Caribbean," *Bloomberg*, April 24, 2014, https://www.bloomberg.com/news/articles/2014-04-24/john-paulson-says-puerto-rico-to-become-singapore-of-caribbean.

282 "Governor invites Spanish firms to invest in Puerto Rico," *El Economista*, June 17, 2014, https://www.eleconomistaamerica.com/noticias-amp/5871460/Governor-invites-Spanish-firms-to-invest-in-Puerto-Rico.

283 Nick Brown and Tom Hals, "Puerto Rico Debt Crisis Headed for U.S.-style Bankruptcy Resolution," Reuters, July 23, 2014, https://www.reuters.com/article/us-puertorico-debt-analysis-idUSKBN0FS0A420140723.

284 Nick Brown and Tom Hals, "Puerto Rico Balances Budget, But Debt Still Has Island on Brink of Financial Collapse," Associated Press, July 21, 2014.

285 "Puerto Rico Economic Activity Drops to 20-year Low," Reuters, September 2, 2014, https://www.reuters.com/article/usa-puertorico-economy-idUSL1N0R31FA20140902.

286 Kasia Klimasinska, "Puerto Rico Faces 'Difficult Choices Ahead,' U.S. Treasury Says," *Bloomberg*, August 4, 2014, https://www.bloomberg.com/news/articles/2014-08-04/puerto-rico-faces-difficult-choices-ahead-u-s-treasury-says.

287 Michael J. De La Merced and Michael Corkery, "Puerto Rico Hires Supervisor for Utility Restructuring," *New York Times*, September 4, 2014, https://dealbook.nytimes.com/2014/09/04/puerto-rico-said-to-hire-alixpartners-to-lead-restructuring-of-power-authority/.

288 "Amid Its Struggles, Puerto Rico Enjoys Drop in Crime," Associated Press, January 14, 2015.

289 "Más Puertorriqueños Armados," *El Nuevo Día*, June 20, 2014, https://www.elnuevodia.com/noticias/seguridad/nota/maspuertorriquenosarmados-1797480/.

290 "ATF: More Weapons Being Smuggled out of Florida to Puerto Rico," WOFL, September 10, 2014.

291 Benjamín Torres Gotay, "La Campaña Contra Puerto Rico," *El Nuevo Dia*, September 7, 2014, https://blogs.elnuevodia.com/las-cosas-por-su-nombre/2014/09/07/la-campana-contra-puerto-rico/.

292 Eduardo Lalo, *Simone* (Chicago: University of Chicago Press, 2012): 134–135.

293 Michael Corkery, "Judge Threatens Plan for Puerto Rico to Avert Financial Catastrophe," *New York Times*, February 9, 2015, https://dealbook.nytimes.com/2015/02/09/judge-threatens-plan-for-puerto-rico-to-avert-financial-catastrophe/.

294 *Franklin California Tax-Free Trust, et al. v. Commonwealth of Puerto Rico, et al. and Puerto Rico Electric Power Authority (PREPA)*, 805 F.3d 322, Nos. 15-1218, 15-1221, 15-1271, 15-1272, (1st Cir. 2015).

295 Mahler and Confessore, "Billion-Dollar Battle."

296 Stephanie Mencimer, "Tea Party Patriots Investigated: Don't Ask, Don't Tell," *Mother Jones*, February 15, 2011, https://www.motherjones.com/politics/2011/02/tea-party-patriots-investigated-part-two/.

297 Matea Gold, "Tea Party PACs Reap Money for Midterms But Spend Little on Candidates," *Washington Post*, April 26, 2014, https://www.washingtonpost.com/politics/tea-pacs-reap-money-for-midterms-but-spend-little-on-candidates/2014/04/26/0e52919a-cbd6-11e3-a75e-463587891b57_story.html.

298 Mahler and Confessore, "Billion-Dollar Battle."

299 Ibid.

300 Marco Rubio, "Toward A Better Future in Puerto Rico," Medium, September 3, 2015, https://medium.com/@marcorubio/toward-a-better-future-in-puerto-rico-1ba5fb9fc367.

301 Mahler and Confessore, "Billion-Dollar Battle."

302 Ibid.

303 "Puerto Rico in Economic Limbo as Legislators Reject Tax Plan," Associated Press, April 30, 2015.

304 Michael Corkery and Mary Williams Walsh, "Puerto Rico's Governor Says Island's Debts Are 'Not Payable'," *New York Times*, June 28, 2015, https://www.nytimes.com/2015/06/29/business/dealbook/puerto-ricos-governor-says-islands-debts-are-not-payable.html.

305 Danica Coto, "Puerto Rico Braces for Austere Budget amid Cash Shortfall," Associated Press, May 8, 2015.

306 "Protesters Decry Cuts to Puerto Rico University," UPI, May 14, 2015.

307 Lizette Alvarez, "Despair and Anger as Puerto Ricans Cope with Debt Crisis," *New York Times*, July 3, 2015, https://www.nytimes.com/2015/07/04/us/despair-and-anger-as-puerto-ricans-cope-with-debt-crisis.html.

308 Corkery and Walsh, "Island's Debts 'Not Payable.'"

309 Anne O. Krueger, Ranjit Teja, and Andrew Wolfe, *Puerto Rico: A Way Forward*, June 29, 2015.

310 Editorial Board, "Puerto Rico Needs Debt Relief," *New York Times*, July 1, 2015, https://www.nytimes.com/2015/07/02/opinion/puerto-rico-needs-debt-relief.html.

311 Danica Coto, "Economists Say Puerto Rico Needs Right to Bankruptcy Option," Associated Press, June 30, 2015, https://apnews.com/f2ef981bf4e640cd81a3dc871a64f9a1.

312 Rupert Neate, "Hedge Funds tell Puerto Rico: Lay off Teachers and Close Schools to Pay us Back," *The Guardian*, July 28, 2015, https://www.theguardian.com/world/2015/jul/28/hedge-funds-puerto-rico-close-schools-fire-teachers-pay-us-back.

313 Jose Fajgenbaum, Jorge Guzman, Claudio Loser, *For Puerto Rico, There is a Better Way* (Washington D.C.: Centennial Group, July 2015).

314 Neate, "Hedge Funds Tell Puerto Rico."

315 Megan Davies and Jessica DiNapoli, "Puerto Rico Nears Default as Debt Restructuring Beckons," Reuters, July 31, 2015, https://www.reuters.com/article/us-usa-puertorico-default-idUSKCN0Q50DL20150731.

316 Danica Coto, "Misery Deepens for Those in Puerto Rico Who Can't Leave," Associated Press, August 3, 2015.

317 Lizette Alvarez and Abby Goodnough, "Puerto Ricans Brace for Crisis in Health Care," *New York Times*, August 2, 2015, https://www.nytimes.com/2015/08/03/us/health-providers-brace-for-more-cuts-to-medicare-in-puerto-rico.html.

318 Alvarez, "Despair and Anger as Puerto Ricans Cope."

319 "Puerto Rico Closes Dozens of Schools as Economic Woes Deepen," Associated Press, May 14, 2015.

320 Danica Coto, "Parched Caribbean Faces Widespread Drought, Water Shortages," Associated Press, June 24, 2015.

321 Danica Coto, "Once-thriving Puerto Rico mountain town faces economic abyss," Associated Press, September 18, 2015.

322 Michelle Estrada Torres, "Sentencian a Guarionex Candelario a Más de 200 Años de Cárcel por Matanza de Agentes en Ponce," *El Nuevo Día*, December 20, 2016, https://www.elnuevodia.com/noticias/tribunales/nota/sentencianaguarionexcandelarioamasde200anosdecarcel-2273959/.

323 "Puerto Rico 'Very Unlikely' to Avoid Jan.1 Default: Governor," Reuters, December 22, 2015, https://www.reuters.com/article/usa-puertorico-default-idUSL1N14B1X420151222.

324 Mary Williams Walsh, "Puerto Rico Defaults on Its Debt Payments," *New York Times*, January 4, 2016, https://www.nytimes.com/2016/01/05/business/dealbook/puerto-rico-defaults-on-debt-payments.html.

325 Mary Williams Walsh, "Puerto Rico Pleads for Congressional Help as Lawsuits Are Filed," *New York Times*, January 8, 2016, https://www.nytimes.com/2016/01/09/business/dealbook/puerto-rico-governor-pleads-for-congressional-action.html.

326 Walsh, "Puerto Rico Defaults on Its Debt Payments."

327 Kasia Klimasinska, "Congress Grasps for Puerto Rico Rescue as House's Deadline Nears," *Bloomberg*, February 25, 2016, https://www.bloomberg.com/news/articles/2016-02-25/congress-grasps-for-puerto-rico-rescue-as-house-s-deadline-nears.

328 Danica Coto, "Puerto Rico Governor Signs into Law Bill for Debt Moratorium," Associated Press, April 6, 2016.

329 "Hedge Funds Are Suing to Freeze Puerto Rico's Government Bank," Reuters, April 5, 2016.

330 Nick Brown, "Puerto Rico Unveils New Debt Restructuring Proposal," Reuters, April 11, 2016, https://www.reuters.com/article/ us-usa-puertorico-debt-idUSKCN0X81MY.

331 Danica Coto, "Federal Judge Seizes Puerto Rico Govt Funds amid Crisis," Associated Press, April 22, 2016.

332 Daniel Bases, "Puerto Rico Either Gets Legislative Fix or Humanitarian Aid: Congressman," Reuters, May 12, 2016, https://www.reuters.com/article/ us-puertorico-debt-idUSKCN0Y32LW.

333 Michelle Kaske, "Latest Casualty of Puerto Rico Cash Grab is University System," *Bloomberg*, September 22, 2016, https://www.bloomberg.com/news/ articles/2016-09-22/latest-casualty-of-puerto-rico-cash-grab -is-university-system.

334 Danica Coto and Mary Clare Jalonick, "Relief and Anger in Puerto Rico as Congress Acts on Debt," Associated Press, May 20, 2016.

335 Danica Coto, "Report Questions whether Puerto Rico Debt Issued Illegally," Associated Press, June 2, 2016, https://apnews.com/ 690cb36603d84c7d8a1b0c30c13b5f1c.

336 Michelle Kaske, "Puerto Rico Says It Will Default Even with Congressional Aid," *Bloomberg*, June 29, 2016, https://www.bloomberg.com/news/arti- cles/2016-06-29/puerto-rico-says-it-will-default-even-with-congressional-help.

337 Russell Berman, "A Vote to Save Puerto Rico from Default," *The Atlantic*, June 29, 2016, https://www.theatlantic.com/politics/ archive/2016/06/a-vote-to-save-puerto-rico-from-default/489323/.

338 David Weigel, "Sanders Opposes Puerto Rico Bill in Test of His Post-Campaign Clout," *Washington Post*, June 28, 2016, https://www.washingtonpost.com/ news/post-politics/wp/2016/06/28/sanders-opposes-puerto-rico-bill-in-test-of -his-post-campaign-clout/?utm_term=.244cca161ccd.

339 Berman, "A Vote to Save Puerto Rico From Default."

340 Heather Long, "Puerto Rico Makes Historic Default," CNN, July 1, 2016, https://money.cnn.com/2016/07/01/investing/puerto-rico-defaults -general-obligation-bonds/index.html.

341 Steven Mufson, "White House Names Seven to Puerto Rico Oversight Board," *Washington Post*, August 31, 2016, https://www.washingtonpost.com/business/ economy/white-house-names-seven-to-puerto-rico-oversight -board/2016/08/31/9cee9376-6f8b-11e6-9705-23e51a2f424d_story. html?utm_term=.780e74ac876f.

342 Nick Brown, "Puerto Rico Oversight Board Wants Lawsuits to Remain Frozen," Reuters, October 21, 2016, https://www.reuters.com/article/ us-puertorico-debt-litigation-idUSKCN12L2RL.

343 "Puerto Rico Pledges $65M to Improve Public Housing Access," Associated Press, October 21, 2016.

344 "Protests Erupt in Puerto Rico over Control Board Meeting," Associated Press, November 18, 2016.

345 Danica Coto, "Puerto Rico Governor Defies New Federal Control Board," Associated Press, November 21, 2016, https://apnews.com/ d45ab63cfc2a484db45e87bcb6dafdef.

346 "Rosselló Diseña Medicamentos en China," *El Nuevo Día*, March 4, 2016, https://www.elnuevodia.com/noticias/politica/nota/ rossellodisenamedicamentosenchina-2169936/.

347 Spalding and Levin, "Puerto Rico's Governor Has to Clean Up His Dad's Mess."

348 Eva Lloréns Vélez, "Fiscal Board Chairman: Extent of Puerto Rico Crisis Justifies New Executive Director Salary," *Caribbean Business*, March 23, 2017, https://caribbeanbusiness.com/oversight-board-appoints-natalie-jaresko -as-executive-director/.

349 Danica Coto, "Puerto Rico Faces Bank Closure, Privatizations amid Crisis," Associated Press, April 28, 2017, https://apnews.com/ ef1bf0636dce4a7fadab9f56329638a2.

350 Danica Coto, "Puerto Rico Pushes to Privatize Public Services," Associated Press, April 20, 2017, https://apnews.com/4cff0e3e92a945cfa68b9812440cc83c.

351 Danica Coto, "Puerto Ricans Protest on May Day as Debt Deadline Nears," Associated Press, May 1, 2017, https://apnews.com/cd78f928d039406bb48bb5 d4d5d60572.

352 Danica Coto, "Puerto Rico Hit with Lawsuit after Litigation Freeze Expires," Associated Press, May 2, 2017, https://apnews.com/ 5a9b1c2db44a49feae5ecd506d64f69d.

353 "Rosselló Destituye a Varios Miembros del Instituto de Estadísticas," *El Nuevo Día*, July 21, 2017, https://www.elnuevodia.com/negocios/economia/nota/ rossellodestituyeavariosmiembrosdelinstitutodeestadisticas-2342425/.

354 Nicole Acevedo, "Puerto Rico's Government, Independent Agency Clash," NBC News, February 1, 2019, https://www.nbcnews.com/news/latino/ puerto-rico-s-government-independent-agency-clash-n965531.

355 Danica Coto, "Puerto Rico to Close 179 Public Schools amid Crisis," Associated Press, May 5, 2017, https://apnews.com/ef5de9ccefe4419aaadc8ba7b791e373.

356 Frances Robles, "Puerto Rico's University Is Paralyzed by Protests and Facing Huge Cuts," *New York Times*, May 25, 2017, https://www.nytimes.com/2017/05/25/us/puerto-ricos-university-is-paralyzed-by-protests-and-facing-huge-cuts.html.

357 Robles, "Puerto Rico's University Paralyzed."

358 Danica Coto, "Outages Increase as Puerto Rico Company Crumbles amid Crisis," Associated Press, April 11, 2017, https://apnews.com/084ee9b96fe04ef890affe33075fbe24.

359 Danica Coto, "Puerto Rico Families Fight, Flee a Surge in Foreclosures," Associated Press, June 21, 2017, https://apnews.com/d08c6338fe334b42b39b8035119c68ad.

360 Coto, "Puerto Rico Families Fight, Flee."

361 Frances Robles, "23% of Puerto Ricans Vote in Referendum, 97% of Them for Statehood," *New York Times*, June 11, 2017, https://www.nytimes.com/2017/06/11/us/puerto-ricans-vote-on-the-question-of-statehood.html.

362 Richard J. Pasch, Andrew B. Penny, and Robbie Berg, *National Hurricane Center: Tropical Cyclone Report: Hurricane Maria (AL152017)*, National Oceanic and Atmospheric Administration and the National Weather Service, April 10, 2018, https://www.nhc.noaa.gov/data/tcr/AL152017_Maria.pdf.

363 Will Worley, "Maria: Dominica PM Gives Terrifying Account of Being at 'Complete Mercy' of a Category 5 Hurricane," *The Independent*, September 19, 2017, https://www.independent.co.uk/news/world/americas/maria-latest-updates-dominica-prime-minister-rossevelt-skerrit-hurricane-category-5-account-a7954616.html.

364 Jorge Figueroa Loza, "Yabucoa pide ayuda a gritos," *Primera Hora*, September 21, 2017, https://www.primerahora.com/noticias/policia-tribunales/nota/yabucoapideayudaagritos-1246772/.

365 Eduardo Cintrón, in discussion with the author, Guayama, PR, September 2018.

366 Karinna D. Sostre Vicario, "Punta Figuera ya No Existe," *Primera Hora*, October 11, 2017, https://www.primerahora.com/noticias/puerto-rico/nota/puntafiguerayanoexiste-1250279/.

367 Benjamín Torres Gotay, "María Deja sin Casa a Miles de Personas," *El Nuevo Día*, October 16, 2017, https://www.elnuevodia.com/noticias/locales/nota/mariadejasincasaamilesdepersonas-2366327/.

368 Pedro Bosque Pérez, "Reportan Ocho Personas Ahogadas en Toa Baja," *El Nuevo Día*, September 21, 2017, https://www.elnuevodia.com/noticias/locales/nota/reportanochopersonasahogadasentoabaja-2359580/.

369 Danica Coto, "Maria Destroys Homes, Triggers Flooding in Puerto Rico," Associated Press, September 20, 2017, https://www.apnews.com/5f2002103e2f42e4916efeda88d0e511.

370 "Alud de Tierra Cobra la Vida de Tres Hermanas en Utuado," *El Nuevo Día*, September 21, 2017, https://www.elnuevodia.com/noticias/locales/nota/aluddetierracobralavidadetreshermanasenutuado-2359462/.

371 Wilma Maldonado Arrigoitia, "Aislado el Barrio San Lorenzo," *El Nuevo Día*, October 25, 2017, https://www.elnuevodia.com/noticias/locales/nota/aisladoelbarriosanlorenzo-2368702/.

372 Danica Coto, "Official: Hurricane Maria set Puerto Rico Back Decades," Associated Press, September 24, 2017, https://apnews.com/251a47c7bbec4c11b82e21edcdf47316.

373 "Inminente la Ruptura de la Represa del Lago Guajataca," *Primera Hora*, September 22, 2017, https://www.primerahora.com/noticias/puerto-rico/nota/inminenteelcolapsodelarepresadeguajataca-1246891/.

374 Frances Robles and Luis Ferré-Sadurní, "Puerto Rico's Agriculture and Farmers Decimated by Maria," *New York Times*, September 24, 2017, https://www.nytimes.com/2017/09/24/us/puerto-rico-hurricane-maria-agriculture-.html.

375 "Puerto Rico Lost $43 Billion after Hurricane Maria, According to Govt. Report," Associated Press, December 4, 2018.

376 Danica Coto, "Maria Destroys Homes, Triggers Flooding in Puerto Rico," Associated Press, September 20, 2017.

377 Benjamín Torres Gotay, "Devastada la Isla por el Golpe de María," *El Nuevo Día*, September 21, 2017, https://www.elnuevodia.com/noticias/locales/nota/devastadalaislaporelgolpedemaria-2359346/.

378 Coto, "Official: Hurricane Maria Set Puerto Rico Back Decades."

379 Ibid.

380 Danica Coto, "Dam Failing as Scope of Puerto Rico's Disaster Becomes Clear," *Associated Press*, September 22, 2017, https://apnews.com/fb547f6a316f4bdc8c226acac09e2426.

381 Danica Coto, "Puerto Ricans Hunt for Precious Wi-Fi and Cell Signals," *Associated Press*, September 24, 2017, https://apnews.com/ff7aa7a71ab94b8a80442c96e13043a7.

382 Eduardo Cintrón, in discussion with the author, Guayama, PR, September 2018.

383 Amanda Holpuch, "Life or Death as Puerto Rico's Older People Go Without Essentials," *The Guardian*, October 3, 2017, https://www.theguardian.com/world/2017/oct/03/puerto-rico-elderly-hurricane-victims.

384 Luis Ferré-Sadurní, Frances Robles, and Lizette Alvarez, "'This Is Like in War': A Scramble to Care for Puerto Rico's Sick and Injured," *New York Times*, September 24, 2017, https://www.nytimes.com/2017/09/26/us/puerto-rico-hurricane-healthcare-hospitals.html.

385 Mike Tighe, "La Crosse Doctor, Back from Puerto Rico, Suspects Hundreds More Dead," *La Crosse Tribune*, October 11, 2017, https://lacrossetribune.com/news/local/la-crosse-doctor-back-from-puerto-rico-suspects-hundreds-more/article_9482721e-bcd0-55b7-a0da-ee92290f8ff1.html.

386 Abby Phillip et al., "Lost Weekend: How Trump's Time at His Golf Club Hurt the Response to Maria," *Washington Post*, September 29, 2017, https://www.washingtonpost.com/politics/lost-weekend-how-trumps-time-at-his-golf-club-hurt-the-response-to-maria/2017/09/29/ce92ed0a-a522-11e7-8c37-e1d99ad6aa22_story.html.

387 Abby Phillip, "Trump Trades Insults with 'Madman' North Korean Leader Kim Jong Un," *Washington Post*, September 22, 2017, https://www.washingtonpost.com/news/post-politics/wp/2017/09/22/trump-warns-that-madman-north-korean-leader-kim-jong-un-will-be-tested/.

388 Jeremy Gottlieb and Mark Maske, "Roger Goodell Responds to Trump's Call to 'Fire' NFL Players Protesting During National Anthem," *Washington Post*, September 23, 2017, https://www.washingtonpost.com/news/early-lead/wp/2017/09/22/donald-trump-profanely-implores-nfl-owners-to-fire-players-protesting-national-anthem/?utm_term=.b5fb71fb3d76.

389 Chris Gilette, "In Hurricane-Hit Puerto Rico, a Stunning Silence," *Associated Press*, October 1, 2017, https://apnews.com/4590c0a86dc7473589a71e15e3b05181.

390 Phillip et al., "Lost Weekend."

391 Ibid.

392 "Latest: US Not Waiving Foreign Ship Restrictions for PR," Associated Press, September 25, 2017.

393 Ferré-Sadurní, Robles, and Alvarez, "'This Is Like in War.'"

394 Ben Fox, "Water and Some Food Scarce as Puerto Rico Emerges from Storm," Associated Press, September 26, 2017.

395 Omayra Gonzalez and José A. Delgado Robles, "El Alcalde de Rincón Urge al Gobierno que Lleve Agua a su Municipio," *El Nuevo Día*, September 24, 2017, https://www.elnuevodia.com/noticias/locales/nota/elalcalderinconurgealgobiernoquelleveaguaasumunicipio-2360076/.

396 Nydia Bauzá, "El Alcalde de Río Grande Clama por Asistencia del Gobierno Central," *El Nuevo Día*, September 22, 2017, https://www.elnuevodia.com/noticias/locales/nota/elalcalderiograndeclamaporasistenciadelgobiernocentral-2359826/.

397 Femmy Irizarry Álvarez, "Alcalde de San Germán Solicita Agilidad al Gobierno ante la Emergencia," *El Nuevo Día*, September 30, 2017, https://www.elnuevodia.com/noticias/locales/nota/alcaldedesangermansolicitaagilidadalgobiernoantelaemergencia-2362027/.

398 Ben Fox and Danica Coto, "Scope of Puerto Rico Damage So Wide that US Aid Hard to See," Associated Press, September 27, 2017.

399 Danica Coto, "A Year after Maria, Puerto Rican Kidney Patients Fear Death," Associated Press, September 19, 2018.

400 Ben Fox, "Now Even Money Is Running Out in Storm-Hit Puerto Rico," Associated Press, September 28, 2017.

401 Dave Graham and Robin Respaut, "In Puerto Rico, a Radio Voice of Calm in the Storm," Reuters, September 28, 2017, https://www.reuters.com/article/us-usa-puertorico-radio/in-puerto-rico-a-radio-voice-of-calm-in-the-storm-idUSKCN1C30HQ.

402 Niraj Chokshi, "Trump Waives Jones Act for Puerto Rico, Easing Hurricane Aid Shipments," *New York Times*, September 28, 2017, https://www.nytimes.com/2017/09/28/us/jones-act-waived.html.

403 Franco Ordoñez and Alex Daugherty, "Trump Races to Catch Up as Puerto Rico Crisis Escalates," *Miami Herald*, September 28, 2017, https://www.miamiherald.com/news/politics-government/article175867361.html.

404 Phillip et al., "Lost Weekend."

405 Steven Mufson et al., "Small Montana Firm Lands Puerto Rico's Biggest Contract to Get the Power Back On," *Washington Post*, October 23, 2017, https://www.washingtonpost.com/national/small-montana-firm-lands-puerto-ricos-biggest-contract-to-get-the-power-back-on/2017/10/23/31cccc3e-b4d6-11e7-9e58-e6288544af98_story.html.

406 Frances Robles and Deborah Acosta, "Puerto Rico Cancels Whitefish Energy Contract to Rebuild Power Lines," *New York Times*, October 29, 2017, https://www.nytimes.com/2017/10/29/us/whitefish-cancel-puerto-rico.html.

407 Keith Wagstaff, "The Mayor of Puerto Rico's Capital Can't Believe this Tiny Firm's $300 Million Contract," Mashable, October 25, 2017, https://mashable.com/2017/10/25/whitefish-puerto-rico-carmen-yulin-cruz/.

408 Ellen Mitchell, "Not Enough Troops, Equipment in Puerto Rico, Says General in Charge of Relief," *The Hill*, September 29, 2017, https://thehill.com/policy/defense/353137-not-enough-troops-equipment-in-puerto-rico-says-general-in-charge-of-relief.

409 Daniel Victor, "San Juan Mayor on Hurricane Response," *New York Times*, September 29, 2017, https://www.nytimes.com/2017/09/29/us/san-juanmayor.html.

410 Donald Trump (@realDonaldTrump), Twitter, September 30, 2017, https://twitter.com/realdonaldtrump/status/914087234869047296?.

411 Peter Baker, "Trump Lashes Out at Puerto Rico Mayor Who Criticized Storm Response," *New York Times*, September 30, 2017, https://www.nytimes.com/2017/09/30/us/politics/trump-puerto-rico-mayor.html.

412 David Nakamura and Ashley Parker, "It Totally Belittled the Moment: Many Look Back in Dismay at Trump's Tossing of Paper Towels in Puerto Rico," *Washington Post*, September 13, 2018, https://www.washingtonpost.com/politics/it-totally-belittled-the-moment-many-look-back-in-anger-at-trumps-tossing-of-paper-towels-in-puerto-rico/2018/09/13/8a3647d2-b77e-11e8-a2c5-3187f427e253_story.html?utm_term=.b8f27b05b8f2.

413 Kathryn Watson, "President Trump's Puerto Rico Visit," CBS News, October 3, 2017, https://www.cbsnews.com/live-news/president-trumps-puerto-rico-visit-live-updates/.

414 Arelis R. Hernandez and Jenna Johnson, "A Tale of Two Puerto Ricos: What Trump Saw—and What He Didn't," *Washington Post*, October 4, 2017, https://www.washingtonpost.com/politics/a-tale-of-two-puerto-ricos-what-trump-saw--and-what-he-didnt/2017/10/04/2eeee62e-a8b9-11e7-850e-2bdd-1236be5d_story.html.

415 Watson, "Trump's Puerto Rico Visit."

416 Danica Coto, "In Hard-Hit Puerto Rico Neighborhood, No Sign of Federal Aid," Associated Press, October 3 2017, https://apnews.com/9bdf491e435043e3ad717975e6f4a8c1.

417 US Environmental Protection Agency, "EPA Hurricane Maria Update for Wednesday, October 11th," October 11, 2017.

418 Hernandez and Johnson, "A Tale of Two Puerto Ricos."

419 Juan Ruiz-Robles, in discussion with author, San Juan, PR, September 2018.

420 Marga Parés Arroyo, "Atribuyen Muertes a Enfermedad Infecciosa que Transmite el Ratón," *El Nuevo Día*, October 9, 2017, https://www.elnuevodia.com/noticias/locales/nota/atribuyenmuertesaenfermedadinfecciosaquetransmiteelraton-2364342/.

421 John D. Sutter, CNN, "Records Suggest Puerto Rico Saw a Leptospirosis Outbreak after Hurricane Maria, but Officials Won't Call It that," *The LaCross Tribune*, July 3, 2018, https://lacrossetribune.com/news/national/records-suggest-puerto-rico-saw-a-leptospirosis-outbreak-after-hurricane/article_e5caddb0-da6d-513e-be56-5a9c6d153cf7.html.

422 Parija Kavilanz, "Doctors in Puerto Rico: 'Reality here is Post-Apocalyptic,'" CNN, October 17, 2017, https://money.cnn.com/2017/10/17/news/economy/puerto-rico-hurricane-recovery-doctors/index.html.

423 Leysa Caro Gonzalez, "Viven Rodeados de Animales Muertos en Añasco," *El Nuevo Día*, October 4, 2017, https://www.elnuevodia.com/noticias/locales/nota/vivenrodeadosdeanimalesmuertosenanasco-2362970/.

424 Michelle Estrada Torres, "La Alimentación es Prioridad en Coamo," *Primera Hora*, October 9, 2017, https://www.primerahora.com/noticias/puerto-rico/nota/laalimentacionesprioridadencoamo-1250059/.

425 Pablo Venes, "Starving Puerto Rican Towns Sharing Food, Eating Plants, and Waiting for FEMA," *Daily Beast*, October 10, 2017, https://www.thedailybeast.com/starving-puerto-rican-towns-sharing-food-eating-plants-and-waiting-for-fema.

426 Benjamín Torres Gotay, "María Deja sin Casa a Miles de Personas," *El Nuevo Día*, October 16, 2017, https://www.elnuevodia.com/noticias/locales/nota/mariadejasincasaamilesdepersonas-2366327/.

427 Donald Trump (@realDonaldTrump), Twitter, October 12, 2017, https://twitter.com/realdonaldtrump/status/918432809282342912?.

428 Laura Sullivan, "FEMA Blamed Delays in Puerto Rico On Maria; Agency Records Tell Another Story," National Public Radio, June 14, 2018, https://www.npr.org/2018/06/14/608588161/fema-blamed-delays-in-puerto-rico-on-maria-agency-records-tell-another-story.

429 Ben Fox, "Many in Puerto Rico Still Under Tarps as Storm Threat Looms," Associated Press, June 20, 2018.

430 Frances Robles, "FEMA Was Sorely Unprepared for Puerto Rico Hurricane, Report Says," *New York Times*, July 12, 2018, https://www.nytimes.com/2018/07/12/us/fema-puerto-rico-maria.html.

431 Frances Robles, "Containers of Hurricane Donations Found Rotting in Puerto Rico Parking Lot," *New York Times*, August 10, 2018, https://www.nytimes.com/2018/08/10/us/puerto-rico-aid.html.

432 José Andrés, in phone interview with author, October 2017.

433 "Le da Igual," from the 2015 album *Le da Igual* by Cultura Profética.

434 For a full account of the US response to Haiti's earthquake, please see my book, *Haiti Will Not Perish: A Recent History* (London: Zed Books, 2017).

435 Joanisabel González, "Rosselló Reafirma que su Plan es Restablecer el Sistema Eléctrico," *El Nuevo Día*, October 18, 2017, https://www.elnuevodia.com/noticias/locales/nota/rosselloreafirmaquesuplanesrestablecerelsistemaelectrico-2366959/.

436 Danica Coto, "Puerto Rico Still Stumbles in the Dark a Month after Maria," Associated Press, October 19, 2017, https://apnews.com/b516c391a7744f818747755e5fea962a.

437 Ricardo Cortés Chico, "La AAA Hace Malabares para Tratar el Agua Usada," *El Nuevo Día*, December 26, 2017, https://www.elnuevodia.com/noticias/locales/nota/laaaahacemalabaresparatratarelaguausada-2384996/.

438 Marga Parés Arroyo, "Fallas Constantes en Sistema Eléctrico Ponen en Peligro a Centro Médico," *El Nuevo Día*, October 23, 2017, https://www.elnuevodia.com/noticias/locales/nota/fallasconstantesensistemaelectricoponenenpeligroacentromedico-2368121/.

439 Robles and Acosta, "Puerto Rico Cancels Whitefish Energy Contract.

440 Robles and Acosta, "Puerto Rico Cancels Whitefish."

441 Richard Cowan, "Puerto Rico Utility Says its Boss is Too Busy for Washington Hearing," Reuters, November 7, 2017, https://www.reuters.com/article/usa-puertorico-power-idUSL1N1ND0Y5.

442 Patricia Guadalupe, "Congressional Committees Slam Puerto Rico Officials Over Controversial Energy Contract," NBC News, November 14, 2017, https://www.nbcnews.com/storyline/puerto-rico-crisis/congressional-committees-slam-puerto-rico-officials-over-controversial-energy-contract-n820811.

443 Phil McCausland, "Ricardo Ramos, embattled head of Puerto Rico's power utility, resigns," NBC News, November 17, 2017, https://www.nbcnews.com/storyline/puerto-rico-crisis/ricardo-ramos-embattled-head-puerto-rico-s-power-utility-resigns-n821881.

444 The Editorial Board, "Puerto Rico's Second-Class Treatment on Food Aid," *New York Times*, November 9, 2017, https://www.nytimes.com/2017/11/09/opinion/puerto-rico-food-aid.html.

445 Mary Williams Walsh, "In Puerto Rico, Law Passed for Fiscal Crisis Hampers Storm Recovery," *New York Times*, November 16, 2017, https://www.nytimes.com/2017/11/16/business/dealbook/puerto-rico-promesa-hurricane.html.

446 Natalie Jaresko, Executive Director FOMB, *Written Testimony of Natalie Jaresko Executive Director Financial Oversight and Management Board for Puerto Rico*, House Committee on Natural Resources, November 7, 2017, https://media.noticel.com/o2com-noti-media-us-east-1/document_dev/2019/05/02/Ms.%20Jaresko%20-%20Testimony%20-%20FC%20Ov%20Hrg%205.2.19%20PROMESA_1556807479877_38269606_ver1.0.pdf.

447 The Editorial Board, "No more excuses. Puerto Rico needs help," *Washington Post*, January 5, 2018, https://www.washingtonpost.com/opinions/no-more-excuses-puerto-rico-needs-help/2018/01/05/8dd307a8-f245-11e7-b390-a36dc3fa2842_story.html.

448 Benjamín Torres Gotay, "El huracán detuvo el tiempo en Morovis," *El Nuevo Día*, December 3, 2017, https://www.elnuevodia.com/noticias/locales/nota/elhuracandetuvoeltiempoenmorovis-2379170/.

449 Jaclyn De Jesús, in discussion with author, May 2019.

450 Teo Freytes, in discussion with author, May 2019.

451 Molly Hennessy-Fiske, "In one Puerto Rican nursing home, a struggle to get power and keep patients alive," *Los Angeles Times*, October 1, 2017, https://www.latimes.com/nation/la-na-puerto-rico-healthcare-20170930-story.html.

452 Danica Coto, "Needs go unmet 6 months after Maria hit Puerto Rico," Associated Press, March 20, 2018, https://www.apnews.com/de367742d0c440de85e4b6cb107973d4.

453 Marga Parés Arroyo, "Suben los suicidios," *El Nuevo Día*, October 3, 2017, https://www.elnuevodia.com/noticias/locales/nota/subenlossuicidios-2362565/.

454 Alex Figueroa Cancel, "Aumentan los suicidios en el 2017," *El Nuevo Día*, February 20, 2018, https://www.elnuevodia.com/noticias/seguridad/nota/aumentanlossuicidiosenel2017-2400243/.

455 "Seis suicidios este fin de semana," *Primera Hora*, September 10, 2018, https://www.primerahora.com/noticias/puerto-rico/nota/seissuicidiosestefindesemana-1301555/.

456 Frances Robles et al., "Official Toll in Puerto Rico: 64. Actual Deaths May Be 1,052," *New York Times*, December 9, 2017, https://www.nytimes.com/interactive/2017/12/08/us/puerto-rico-hurricane-maria-death-toll.html.

457 Frances Robles, "Puerto Rican Government Acknowledges Hurricane Death Toll of 1,427," *New York Times*, August 9, 2018, https://www.nytimes.com/2018/08/09/us/puerto-rico-death-toll-maria.html.

458 *Transformation and Innovation in the Wake of Devastation: An Economic and Disaster Recovery Plan for Puerto Rico* (San Juan, PR: Government of Puerto Rico, August 2018).

459 Milken Institute of Public Health in collaboration with University of Puerto Rico Graduate School of Public Health, *Ascertainment of the Estimated Excess Mortality from Hurricane Maria in Puerto Rico* (Washington, DC: George Washington University, August 2018).

460 Natasha Kishore, et al., "Mortality in Puerto Rico after Hurricane Maria," *New England Journal of Medicine*, no. 379 (July 12, 2018): 162–170.

461 Amnesty International, "USA: Policy of Separating Children from Parents is Nothing Short of Torture," June 18, 2018, https://www.amnesty.org/en/latest/news/2018/06/usa-family-separation-torture/.

462 Mark Follman, "Trump's 'Enemy of the People' Rhetoric Is Endangering Journalists' Lives," *Mother Jones*, September 13, 2018, https://www.motherjones.com/politics/2018/09/trump-enemy-of-the-people-media-threats/.

463 Adam Taylor, "The North Korean Human Rights Issue Stalking the Singapore Summit," *Washington Post*, June 11, 2018, https://www.washingtonpost.com/news/worldviews/wp/2018/06/11/the-north-korean-human-rights-issue-stalking-the-singapore-summit/.

464 Betsy Klein and Meagan Vazquez, "Trump Falsely Claims Nearly 3,000 Americans in Puerto Rico 'Did Not Die'," CNN, September 14, 2018, https://www.cnn.com/2018/09/13/politics/trump-puerto-rico-death-toll/index.html.

465 Jordan Fabian, "Trump Says Puerto Rico Death Toll Inflated by Democrats," *The Hill*, September 13, 2018, https://thehill.com/homenews/administration/406446-trump-questions-death-toll-of-hurricane-in-puerto-rico.

466 Klein and Vazquez, "Trump Falsely Claims."

467 Mabel M. Figueroa Pérez, "Familiares de víctimas fatales del huracán se sienten ofendidos por expresiones de Trump," *El Nuevo Día*, September 14, 2018, https://www.elnuevodia.com/noticias/locales/nota/familiaresdevictimasfatales-delhuracansesientenofendidosporexpresionesdetrump-2447149/.

468 John Wagner and Joel Achenbach, "Trump is Rebuked after Questioning Number of Deaths Attributed to Hurricane Maria," *Washington Post*, September 13, 2018, https://www.washingtonpost.com/politics/trump-questions-number-of-deaths-attributed-to-hurricane-maria-falsely-says-democrats-created-a-higher-count-to-make-him-look-bad/2018/09/13/9519308a-b73b-11e8-a7b5-adaaa5b2a57f_story.html.

469 Charley E Willison et al., "Quantifying Inequities in US Federal Response to Hurricane Disaster in Texas and Florida Compared with Puerto Rico," *BMJ Global Health* 4, no.1 (January 2019), https://gh.bmj.com/content/4/1/e001191.

470 Julia de Burgos, "Rio Grande de Loíza," *Song of the Simple Truth: The Complete Poems of Julia de Burgos* (Willimantic, CT: Curbstone Press, 1997): 8.

471 "'If anyone can hear us ... help' Puerto Rico's mayors describe widespread devastation from Hurricane Maria," *Washington Post*, September 23, 2017.

472 José Martorell, in discussion with author, October 2017.

473 Adrian Florido, "FEMA To End Food and Water Aid For Puerto Rico." National Public Radio, January 29, 2018, https://www.npr.org/sections/thetwo-way/2018/01/29/581511023/fema-to-end-food-and-water-aid-for-puerto-rico.

474 "New data shows 4 percent drop in Puerto Rico population since Maria," Associated Press, April 17, 2019, https://apnews.com/df63a2f9186a4eaaaa531d69d59adf4e.

475 Danica Coto, "Puerto Rico Moves to Privatize Troubled Power Company," Associated Press, January 22, 2018, https://apnews.com/5221fe5a9b1247e1ad1af0e1c35bf5e6.

476 Michael Weissenstein, "Puerto Rico Grid 'Teetering' Despite $3.8 Billion Repair Job," Associated Press, May 31, 2018, https://apnews.com/fa210cd1434c4d909e6030c7da884bce.

477 Michael Weissenstein and Danica Coto, "Turmoil slows rebuilding of Puerto Rico's power grid," Associated Press, July 19, 2018, https://apnews.com/11893d2477e04e7f9b9c8befbea295ad.

478 Nick Brown, "Puerto Rico's PREPA Gets Energy Industry Veteran Higgins as New CEO," Reuters, March 20, 2018, https://www.reuters.com/article/us-puertorico-prepa-ceo-idUSKBN1GW32G.

479 Eva Lloréns Vélez, "Puerto Rico Power Company Chairman Defends New CEO's Pay," *Caribbean Business*, March 22, 2018, https://caribbeanbusiness.com/puerto-rico-power-company-chairman-defends-new-ceos-pay/.

480 Danica Coto, "Puerto Ricans grab machetes, shovels to help restore power," Associated Press, February 7, 2018, https://www.apnews.com/394fe201adf64649a92fe8e9b82000e1.

481 Patricia Mazzei, "Protest in Puerto Rico Over Austerity Measures Ends in Tear Gas," *New York Times*, May 1, 2018, https://www.nytimes.com/2018/05/01/us/puerto-rico-protests.html.

482 Andrew Scurria, "Puerto Rico Power Utility CEO Resigns After Less Than Four Months on Job," *Wall Street Journal*, July 11, 2018, https://www.wsj.com/articles/puerto-rico-power-utility-ceo-resigns-after-less-than-4-months-on-job-1531328679.

483 Karen Pierog, "Puerto Rico Governor Names New Utility Head after Board Members Quit," Reuters, July 18, 2018, https://www.reuters.com/article/usa-puertorico-prepa/update-1-puerto-rico-governor-names-new-utility-head-after-board-members-quit-idUSL1N1UE1EV.

484 Simone Baribeau, "Puerto Rico Oversight Board Pushes For Secrecy," *Forbes*, June 18, 2018, https://www.forbes.com/sites/debtwire/2018/06/18/puerto-rico-oversight-board-pushes-for-secrecy/.

485 Danica Coto, "Puerto Rico Faces Austerity Measures amid Budget Wrangling," Associated Press, June 29, 2018, https://www.apnews.com/0ad6c5ab85f740f187b8acb6c26ed084.

486 José A. Delgado Robles, "La Junta de Supervisión Fiscal firma un nuevo contrato en Washington," *El Nuevo Día*, April 14, 2019, https://www.elnuevodia.com/noticias/locales/nota/lajuntadesupervisionfiscalfirmaunnuevocontratoenwashington-2487922/.

487 Andrew Rice with Luis J. Valentín Ortiz, "The McKinsey Way to Save an Island," *New York* magazine, April 17, 2019, http://nymag.com/intelligencer/2019/04/mckinsey-in-puerto-rico.html.

488 Andrew Rice with Luis J. Valentín Ortiz, "McKinsey: Puerto Rico Bondholder and Fiscal Board's Lead Adviser," Centro de Periodismo Investigativo, December 12, 2018, http://periodismoinvestigativo.com/2018/12/mckinsey-puerto-rico-bondholder-and-fiscal-boards-lead-adviser/.

489 José A. Delgado Robles, "La Junta de Supervisión Fiscal Firma un Nuevo Contrato en Washington," *El Nuevo Día*, April 14, 2019, https://www.elnuevodia.com/noticias/locales/nota/lajuntadesupervisionfiscalfirmaunnuevocontratoenwashington-2487922/.

490 Danica Coto, "Puerto Rico Governor Rejects Budget in Challenge to Board," Associated Press, July 2, 2018, https://www.apnews.com/aa134f04810b45f193f97d348e3f9549.

491 Luis J. Valentín Ortiz, "Puerto Rico Bankruptcy Judge Upholds Oversight Board Powers Over Gov't," Reuters, August 7, 2018, https://uk.reuters.com/article/uk-usa-puertorico-lawsuit/puerto-rico-bankruptcy-judge-upholds-oversight-board-powers-over-govt-idUKKBN1KS2IP.

492 Danica Coto, "Puerto Rico Senators Deal Blow to Governor amid Budget Clash," Associated Press, July 3, 2018, https://apnews.com/258712ef76ba4a55a7b88514f8747a72.

493 Ortiz, "Bankruptcy Judge Upholds Oversight Board."

494 Luis J. Valentín Ortiz, "Puerto Rico to Get $18.5 Billion to Rebuild Shattered Housing Market," Reuters, April 10, 2018, https://www.reuters.com/article/ us-usa-puertorico-housing/puerto-rico-to-get-18-5-billion-to-rebuild-shattered -housing-market-idUSKBN1HH3IR?il=0.

495 Danica Coto, "Puerto Ricans Fight for Insurance Money a Year after Maria," Associated Press, October 23, 2018.

496 Coto, "Puerto Ricans Fight."

497 Ben Fox, "Many in Puerto Rico still under tarps as storm threat looms," Associated Press, June 20, 2018, https://www.apnews.com/ a99551194b144db490b25c7f0e6d46fd.

498 "Puerto Rico Sues Insurance Companies amid Unresolved Claims," Associated Press, September 18, 2018, https://www.apnews.com/ aca22421b73e4ad8b0bbcd9c78631668.

499 FEMA, email to author, August 30, 2018.

500 Tracey Jan and Josh Dawsey, "HUD's Top Watchdog: Agency Impeded Probe into Puerto Rico Hurricane Aid," *Washington Post*, April 30, 2019, https://www.washingtonpost.com/business/2019/04/30/ huds-top-watchdog-agency-is-impeding-probe-into-puerto-rico-hurricane-aid/.

501 "Gobierno Confirma que no está Listo el Plan de Manejo de Emergencias para todas las Agencias," Centro de Periodismo Investigativo, October 30, 2018, http://periodismoinvestigativo.com/2018/10/gobierno-confirma-que -no-esta-listo-el-plan-de-manejo-de-emergencia-para-todas-las-agencias/.

502 D.R. Reidmiller et al., *Fourth National Climate Assessment: Volume II Impacts, Risks, and Adaptation in the United States* (Washington, DC: US Global Change Research Program, November 2018).

503 Nicole Acevedo, "Puerto Rico's Government, Independent Agency Clash," NBC News, February 1, 2019, https://www.nbcnews.com/news/latino/ puerto-rico-s-government-independent-agency-clash-n965531.

504 CyberNews, "Puerto Rico Statistics Institute's Marazzi resigns," *Caribbean Business*, February 11, 2019, https://caribbeanbusiness.com/ puerto-rico-statistics-institutes-marazzi-resigns/.

505 Luis Valentin Ortiz, "Puerto Rico Creditors End Opposition to Bank Debt Restructuring," Reuters, October 5, 2018, https://www.reuters.com/article/us-usa-puertorico-creditors-idUSKCN1MF2HH.

506 Yalixa Rivera and Jonathan Levin, "Can Crypto, Cannabis, and Nicolas Cage Boost Puerto Rico's Economy?" *Bloomberg*, September 10, 2018, https://www.bloomberg.com/news/articles/2018-09-10/can-crypto-cannabis-and-nicolas-cage-boost-puerto-rico-s-economy.

507 Nellie Bowles, "Making a Crypto Utopia in Puerto Rico," *New York Times*, February 2, 2018, https://www.nytimes.com/2018/02/02/technology/cryptocurrency-puerto-rico.html.

508 Rivera and Levin, "Crypto, Cannabis, and Nicolas Cage."

509 Neil Strauss, "Brock Pierce: The Hippie King of Cryptocurrency," *Rolling Stone*, July 26, 2018, https://www.rollingstone.com/culture/culture-features/brock-pierce-hippie-king-of-cryptocurrency-700213/.

510 John Gorenfeld and Patrick Runkle, November 5, 2007, http://web.archive.org/web/20080117004139/http://radaronline.com/from-the-magazine/2007/11/den_chads_world_marc_collins_rector_1.php.

511 Julian Dibbell, "The Decline and Fall of an Ultra Rich Online Gaming Empire," *Wired*, November 24, 2008, https://www.wired.com/2008/11/ff-ige/.

512 Dibbell, "Decline and Fall."

513 Ibid.

514 Strauss, "Brock Pierce."

515 Dibbell, "Decline and Fall."

516 "Fast Company," *Radar*.

517 Ellie Hall, Nicolás Medina Mora, and David Noriega, "Found: The Elusive Man At The Heart Of The Hollywood Sex Abuse Scandal" *BuzzFeed*, June 26, 2014, https://www.buzzfeednews.com/article/ellievhall/found-the-elusive-man-at-the-heart-of-the-hollywood-sex-abus.

518 Strauss, "Brock Pierce."

519 "Fast Company," *Radar*.

520 Hall, Mora, and Noriega, "Found."

521 Dean Takahashi, "Blockchain Billionaire Brock Pierce on Saving Puerto Rico, Cryptocurrency Games, and Fighting Controversy," *VentureBeat*, October 29, 2018, https://venturebeat.com/2018/10/29/blockchain-billionaire-brock -pierce-interview/.

522 Strauss, "Brock Pierce."

523 Ibid.

524 Ibid.

525 Bowles, "Making a Crypto Utopia in Puerto Rico."

526 Ibid.

527 La Isla Oeste, "Rincoeños cuestiónan el propósito de los cryptosueñit," YouTube video, 4:04, May 21, 2018 https://youtu.be/nwvHylZLMxY.

528 Michael Murray, Facebook video, May 17, 2018, https://www.facebook.com/michael.murray.752861/videos/ pcb.10212430775030958/10212430727829778/?type=3&theater.

529 Tracy Jan et al., "After Butting Heads with Trump Administration, Top HUD Official Departs Agency," *Washington Post*, January 16, 2019, https://www.washingtonpost.com/business/economy/top-hud-officials -departure-follows-disagreements-over-housing-policy-and-puerto-rico -disaster-funds/2019/01/16/e6ba5be4-1839-11e9-9ebf-c5fed1b7a081 _story.html.

530 Antonio S. Pedreira, *Insularismo* (Río Piedras, PR: Editorial Edil, 1934): 111.

531 Pedreira, *Insularismo*, 32.

532 Richard Danielson, "Tampa Shipping Executives Rally Around the Jones Act," *Tampa Bay Times*, March 22, 2019, https://www.tampabay.com/business/ tampa-shipping-executives-rally-around-the-jones-act-an-old-law-facing-a -new-challenge-20190322/.

533 Danielson, "Tampa Shipping Executives Rally Around the Jones Act".

534 Andrew Taylor, "Trump Opposes Further Disaster Aid for Battered Puerto Rico," Associated Press, March 26, 2019, https://www.apnews.com/ df711dcff96a41218161a452340f0325.

535 Emily Cochrane, "Impasse Over Aid for Puerto Rico Stalls Billions in Federal Disaster Relief," *New York Times*, April 1, 2019, https://www.nytimes.com/ 2019/04/01/us/politics/puerto-rico-aid.html.

536 Jacob Pramuk, "Trump Signs $19 Billion Disaster Relief Bill and Says Puerto Rico 'Should Love' Him," *CNBC*, June 6, 2019, https://www.cnbc.com/2019/06/06/trump-signs-natural-disaster-relief-bill-for-puerto-rico-and-states.html.

537 Danica Coto, "Puerto Ricans Decry Austerity, Hurricane Help at Hearing," Associated Press, March 16, 2019, https://apnews.com/1211eb3e68b24c35a994c60973c8de65.

538 Patricia Mazzei, "Hunger and an 'Abandoned' Hospital: Puerto Rico Waits as Washington Bickers," *New York Times*, April 7, 2019, https://www.nytimes.com/2019/04/07/us/puerto-rico-trump-vieques.html.

539 Leysa Caro González, "Las vidas que aún habitan bajo el toldo de FEMA," *El Nuevo Día*, May 18, 2019, https://www.elnuevodia.com/noticias/locales/nota/lasvidasqueaunhabitanbajoeltoldodefema-2494479/.

540 Frances Rosario, "FEMA está atrás y no avanza para los alcaldes," *Primera Hora*, May 20, 2019, https://www.primerahora.com/noticias/gobierno-politica/nota/femaestaatrasynoavanzaparalosalcaldes-1343556/.

541 Pramuk, "Trump Signs $19 Billion Disaster Relief Bill."

542 Aris Folley, "San Juan Mayor Carmen Yulín Cruz Running for Puerto Rico Governor in 2020," *The Hill*, March 22, 2019, https://thehill.com/latino/435352-san-juan-mayor-carmen-yulin-cruz-running-for-puerto-rico-governor-in-2020.

543 Michael Deibert, "Puerto Rico Governor Ousts Treasurer Amid Reported FBI Probe," *Bloomberg*, June 24, 2019, https://www.bloomberg.com/news/articles/2019-06-24/puerto-rico-governor-ousts-treasurer-amid-reported-fbi-probe.

544 Ibid.

545 Alex Figueroa Cancel, "Jefe del FBI Asegura que los Sobornos en el Gobierno Han Ocurrido 'en una Forma Dramática,'" *El Nuevo Día*, June 27, 2019, https://www.elnuevodia.com/noticias/locales/nota/jefedelfbiaseguraquelossobornosenelgobiernohanocurridoenunaformadramatica-2502099/.

546 Deibert, "Puerto Rico Governor Ousts Treasurer."

547 Jonathan Levin and Michael Deibert, "Vitriol Flies in Puerto Rico as FBI is Said to Probe Treasury," *Bloomberg*, June 25, 2019, https://www.bloomberg.com/news/articles/2019-06-25/vitriol-flies-in-puerto-rico-as-fbi-is-said-to-probe-treasury.

548 Levin and Deibert, "Vitriol Flies in Puerto Rico."

549 Michael Deibert and Michelle Kaske, "Ex-Puerto Rico Officials Charged in Corruption Probe," *Bloomberg*, July 10, 2019. https://www.bloomberg.com/news/articles/2019-07-10/ex-puerto-rico-officials-arrested-amid-fbi-probes-el-nuevo-dia?fbclid=IwAR0tCm7lIB9CELfx2qHVqaryEdxNcL2_Y5qUpj1kZIDR05tw3l1NRugE1A8.

550 Nicole Acevedo, "Democratic Debates Didn't Address Puerto Rico Despite Island's Possible Early Primary," NBC, June 28, 2019, https://www.nbcnews.com/news/latino/democratic-debates-didn-t-address-puerto-rico-despite-island-s-n1024401.

ACKNOWLEDGMENTS

IN THE COURSE OF WRITING THIS BOOK, I WAS AIDED BY THE support of those who recognized the value of the work.

On *la isla del encanto* itself, I would like to thank Nydia Alvarado, Daniela María Buscaglia Casares, Joel Cintrón Arbasetti, Victor Díaz and Carmen Rosa Maldonado López, Nydia Meléndez Rivas, Harry Nussbaum and Linda Nussbaum-Ulrich, Juan Ruiz-Robles, and Jacques-Christian Wadestrandt.

Outside of the island, I would like to thank Sylvie Bajeux, Courtney Body, Neil Brandvold, Justin Cappiello, Natasha Del Toro, Carmen Graciela Díaz, David Doherty, Anna Edgerton, Sasha Elliott, Melanie Erker, Meghan Feeks, Carrie Gibson, Daniela Guzmán Peña, Bahare Khodabande, Cassie Leventhal, Charles Manus, Louis-Henri Mars, Kevin McCaffrey, Eirin Mobekk, Keiko Niccolini, Laura Parker, Valentina Pereda, Nomi Prins, Thos Robinson, Huascar Robles, Francesca Romeo, Nikki Roth, Claudia Scalise, Philip Schnell, Mike Stitt, Sutton Stokes, Claire Sturm, Noelle Théard, Jenn Vogtle, Li Wallis, and Douglas Young.

At Apollo Publishers, Julia Abramoff and Alex Merrill were a pleasure to work with. Thank you for believing in this book.

Thank you to my family: my father, Caleb Deibert, and brothers,

Benjamin Deibert and Christopher Deibert.

In addition, I would like to acknowledge and thank the spirits of *los que se fueron*, my grandparents, Joseph and Elizabeth Deibert and James and Leah Breon, and my mother, Jann Marie Deibert.

May fortune smile upon you at long last, Borinquen, and may your beautiful sunsets and the warmth of your people endure, *siempre*.